SHORT CUTS

INTRODUCTIONS TO FILM STUDIES

PSYCHOANALYSIS AND CINEMA

THE PLAY OF SHADOWS

VICKY LEBEAU

WALLFLOWER

LONDON and NEW YORK

A Wallflower Paperback

1004668 145.

First published in Great Britain in 2001 by Wallflower Press
5 Pond Street, Hampstead, London NW3 2PN
www.wallflowerpress.co.uk

A catalogue record for this book is available from the British Library

ISBN 1 903364 19 1

Book Design by Rob Bowden Design

Printed in Great Britain by Biddles Limited, Guildford and King's Lynn

CONTENTS

ACKNOWLEDGEMENTS

My thanks to my research students – in particular, Suzy Gordon, Tanya Horeck, Paul Myerscough, and Matthew Bennett – whose interests in psychoanalysis and cinema have helped to sustain my own; and to the students and faculty associated with the Literature and Visual Culture MA Programme at the University of Sussex. For conversation and support, my thanks to Alan Sinfield, Vincent Quinn, Amber Jacobs, Nick Royle, Laura Marcus, and Michael Payne. David Marriott's critical reading came at a crucial point – my thanks to him. The book could not have been completed without the timely help of Doreen and Gary Lebeau, and John Shire.

INTRODUCTION

On December 28, 1895, cinema begins in the basement of the Grand Café, Boulevard des Capucines, Paris. It is the first public demonstration of what Gustav and Antoine Lumière's new device, the *Cinématographe*, can do: the projection of moving images, of pictures which flicker into life, on screen. It is a strange and spectral world – 'Last night I was in the kingdom of the shadows,' wrote Maxim Gorky in 1896 – and one that sparks a craze for this new way of seeing: the '"living picture" craze', as it will quickly become known. There is a hint of madness in the well-known phrase, as if the spectators who flock to discover this world are 'touched' by what they see, aroused to an 'excitement bordering on terror,' as one journalist was to put it, commenting on the Lumière screenings in 1896 (Gunning 1997: 121). Sometimes, it seems, terror became panic. The Lumières' *L'Arrivée d'un Train en Gare de La Ciotat* is supposed to have had spectators rearing away from the screen, the dread of colliding with the rush of that enormous machine too much for those who succumbed to the hallucination of the image. It moves, and it comes towards you, a movement which is part of the shock of early cinema: the still photograph, the inanimate image, brought to life before the very eyes of the spectators . . . as if in a dream.

Suspended between realism and illusion, cinema comes into a first point of contact with psychoanalysis – Freud's own visionary exploration of shock and dream. 1895 also saw the publication, in Vienna, of Josef Breuer and Sigmund Freud's *Studies on Hysteria*, the book that would open the door to the study of the unconscious life of the mind. Fräulein Anna O., Frau Emmy von N., Miss Lucy R., Katharina, Fräulein Elisabeth von R. – the five women whose stories are told through the *Studies on Hysteria* take Freud, and his readers, into another strange, sometimes distressing, world of illusion and illness. 'An enormous mouse suddenly whisked across my hand in the garden and was gone in a flash,' Frau Emmy von N. tells Freud towards the beginning of her lengthy, often bizarre, treatment with him; 'things kept gliding backwards and forwards' (Freud and Breuer 1895: 72). What is his patient talking about? Freud is not sure. 'An illusion from the play of shadows?' he wonders to himself, trying to account for the fact that, gripped by an image which intrudes upon her mind with all the vividness of reality, Frau Emmy is seeing things which are not there: 'A whole lot of mice were sitting in the trees.'

Cinema and psychoanalysis: part of the long, uneven history of developments in modern art, science and technology, these two powerful ways of seeing and knowing the world appeared together towards the end of the nineteenth century. This book is about some of the subsequent encounters between the two: the seductions of psychoanalysis and cinema as converging, though distinct, ways of talking about dream and desire, image and illusion, memory and shock. It is, of course, a complicated story. Cinema, like psychoanalysis, has its own history, one that can be traced back to the late eighteenth century through a history of visual culture and ideas concerning vision: studies in perception and physiology, say, or in photography and optics.[1] Similarly, Freud's elaboration of psychoanalysis drew upon a range of diverse influences in modern neurology and psychology – as well as the 'unscientific' contributions of literature, myth and the history of the occult.[2] From the beginning of the twentieth century, however, psychoanalysis and cinema have been part of one another's field of influence and understanding. Very quickly, cinema becomes a way of talking about, of picturing, the mind for psychoanalysis – just as the mind becomes one way to consider the mechanism, and fascination, of cinema. 'The movies really play a role of no small significance for us,' wrote Lou Andreas-Salomé towards the end of February 1913, 'and this is not the first time I have thought about this fact' (Andreas-Salomé 1987: 101). Her brief, but tantalising, note on 'Movies' in the journal she kept during her studies in psychoanalysis in Vienna between 1912 and 1913, anticipates a question that will be brought to the fore by attempts to bring psychoanalysis and cinema together: What (if any) is the connection between film and mind? Between the techniques of cinema – its movement, its image, its illusion – and the processes of thought and feeling, dream and imagination which preoccupy psychoanalysis? 'Only the technique of the film permits the rapid sequence of pictures which approximates our own imaginative faculty,' Andreas-Salomé muses in the course of her reflections on the difference between cinema, theatre and photography; 'it might even be said to imitate its erratic ways.'

Cinema, in other words, has a special tie to the life of the mind: approximate, imitative, it is a type of mime of both mind and world. Silent and gestural, cinema can move like the imagination. Breaking free from the confines of photography and theatre, it is unique in its representation of an abundant world in motion ('All the animation of the street,' as Georges Méliès put it in 1895 (cited in Gunning 1997: 119)). It can be difficult, now, to grasp the impact of that animation in the early years of cinema, its importance to an understanding of cinema as a machine of illusion – a 'technique of the imaginary', to borrow the phrase that, decades later, Christian Metz would use to introduce his groundbreaking study of psychoanalysis and cinema (Metz 1982: 3). Nevertheless, a persistent sense that cinema imitates the movement of the mind, that there is a correspondence (however elusive) to be discovered between psyche and cinema, is essential to the approaches explored in this book. 'In the social life of our age,' wrote Metz in 1977, 'the fiction film enters into functional competition with the daydream' – a claim that is going to stake the ground for a psychoanalysis of film as dream, as daydream, as the projection of thought, and wish, on screen. As we will see, Metz played a key role in the development of a new psychoanalytic theory of film through the 1970s and 1980s, but his analogy between film and (day)dream was also attuned to a long tradition in thinking about cinema. 'The film is the art of dream portrayal,' wrote the poet H.D. in 1930, 'and perhaps when we say that we have achieved the definition, the synthesis toward which we have been striving' (Donald et al. 1998: 232).

Commenting on Kenneth Macpherson's experimental film, *Borderline* – 'I was going to take my film into the minds of the people in it,' Macpherson insisted – H.D. was also giving voice to a belief cherished, and promoted, through the early film journal *Close Up*, published from 1927 to 1933. Like H.D., many of the writers (poets, film-makers, psychoanalysts) who contributed to the journal were intrigued by the potential for dialogue between psychoanalysis and film. 'Night dreams, day dreams, fantasies, delirium, are according to Freud direct manifestations of the Unconscious,' wrote L. Saalschutz in 'The Film in its Relation to the Unconscious', published in the July issue of *Close Up* in 1929. 'With these I class the direct visually-excited mass fantasy of the Cinema' (256). It is an emphasis on cinema as the medium able to make visible the intricacies of mental life shared by (amongst others) the psychoanalyst Hanns Sachs. 'The film seems to be a new way of driving mankind to conscious recognition,' he concludes his article on 'Film Psychology' in November 1929, ' ... it shows us clearly and unmistakably things that are to be found in life but that ordinarily escape our notice' (254, 252).

Like a dream, then, film is also an invaluable document, a means to record what might otherwise be lost. Put this way, cinema becomes a form of dreaming in public: the 'transmuted and regulated dream life of the people' as C.J. Pennethorne Hughes was to put it in 1930. It is a rich, and disparate, analogy between film and dream, film and fantasy, film and document – and one that makes its call on psychoanalysis as a very modern form of dream interpretation, a therapy which is going to put fantasy at the heart of its understanding of being and reality. As a 'dream-factory' (to borrow Hortense Powdermaker's phrase) dedicated to the production of illusion and pleasure, as the 'delusion of a man awake' (Metz again), cinema is also a challenge to reading Freud for what he has to say about the idea of dream and delusion in modern culture (Powdermaker 1950; Metz 1982: 109). How does Freud contribute to our understanding of the dream? How does psychoanalysis conceive the role of fantasy –

both pleasure and terror – in our public and private lives? In other words, what happens when Freud's massive reworking of dream and fantasy – a reworking which supports his lifelong preoccupation with mind, illness and culture – is brought to bear on the fascinations of cinema?

So often provocative in its clinical insights into the experience of self, the movement of psychoanalysis outside the analytic situation is not necessarily straightforward. Any attempt to think about the relation between psychoanalysis and cinema comes up against the vexed issue of how to 'apply' psychoanalysis to an object outside of the clinical situation which is its unique domain. In the first place, the intimacy of the speaking-between-two which founds the relation between psychoanalyst and patient makes it easy to think about psychoanalysis as a form of withdrawal from the world – a retreat to the safety of a space in which nothing happens but talk ('Nothing takes place between them,' Freud explained, 'except that they talk to each other' (Freud 1926: 187)). Certainly, psychoanalysis is one way for a culture to recognise an individual's right to have a mind of her own, a private life with the right to speak about that life in private. Perhaps because it began with the wishes, and failures, of sexuality (what Freud described as the 'sexual business'), psychoanalysis has been associated with what is intimate, secret, and personal. At the same time – not least because it works through the dialogue established between analyst and analysand – psychoanalysis is also about the interpersonal: the self as a web of relations forged through the ties of family, work, culture, politics. In fact, part of the purchase of Freud's thinking is its attention to how our earliest ties to the world (people and objects) continue to make themselves felt through the institutions of politics and culture – institutions which are the point of connection between public and private worlds.[3]

From the beginning of his discovery of the unconscious mind, then, Freud was confronted by the fact that the most intimate can also be the most shared, the wayward individualism of internal life can also belong to a culture. One of his first examples is the 'typical dream' – an odd, and complex, topic which forms the core of this book, its attempt to grapple with what it means to use psychoanalysis to think about cinema. 'There are a certain number of dreams,' Freud writes, towards the beginning of *The Interpretation of Dreams*, first published in 1900, 'which almost everyone has dreamt alike and which we are accustomed to assume must have the same meaning for everyone' (Freud 1900: 241). *Oedipus Rex*, the incestuous and parricidal dream of European culture, is his model: the drama of sex and murder in the family supposed to preoccupy us all. But what, precisely, is this notion of a collective dream shared between members of a family, a community, a nation? The idea travels from Freud's *The Interpretation of Dreams* to the descriptions of film as a record of (popular, mass) dreaming that emerge in the course of the twentieth century.

The wager of such a description can be high. 'It is my contention,' wrote Siegfried Kracauer in *From Caligari to Hitler*, 'that through an analysis of the German films deep psychological dispositions predominant in Germany from 1918 to 1933 can be exposed' (Kracauer 1947: v). That is, embedded in the images and narratives of German cinema is a 'secret history' (Kracauer's phrase) which can be used to uncover the deep psychology supporting the rise of Nazism in Germany between the two World Wars. In question, once again, is the profound correspondence between cinema and the (unconscious) mind – a correspondence which extends to both *how* and *what* the mind thinks. Psychoanalytic criticism has been characterised by its attention to both: Kracauer's emphasis on German film as a reflection of the tie between psyche and national-political violence, say, or feminist attention to the sexual politics trafficked by the image of woman in classical, and contemporary, Hollywood cinema. 'Woman as Image, Man as Bearer of the Look' runs the headline in Laura Mulvey's now classic intervention in the psychoanalysis of film (Mulvey 1992: 27).

From this point of view, cinema is something like the royal road to the cultural unconscious; it takes up the place occupied by the dream in Freud's classic account of psychoanalytic interpretation: 'The interpretation of dreams is the royal road to a knowledge of the unconscious activities of the mind' (Freud 1900: 608). Part of the appeal of this approach to film is its promise of a means to psychoanalyse culture – to discover its symptoms in its cinema-dreams. Like the psychoanalyst, the spectator of cinema can become an astute interpreter, a reader of public dreams unreeling before her on screen. As Richard Maltby puts it in his introduction to *Hollywood Cinema*, psychoanalytic approaches to film have been characterised by an insistence that 'movie analysis should be a politically sensitive activity that could contribute to a transformation of wider social relations' (Maltby 1995: 427). A political project, in other words: the psychoanalysis of cinema as a means to social critique, cinema as a 'symptom' of the cultures in which it takes up its place. How psychoanalysis does this remains a troubled question. Do we take psychoanalytic concepts and 'apply' them to a film? Are we looking for the 'unconscious' of cinema? Do psychoanalytic readings give privileged attention to particular themes: sex, death, madness? What are we doing when we read, and look, psychoanalytically?

There are no simple answers to these questions. Psychoanalytic criticism has done all these things (and more). Clearly, however, the encounter between psychoanalysis and cinema depends on the work of interpretation. Psychoanalysis interprets cinema. It recognises the significance of cinema, attempts to understand both its lure and its pathology. But, and crucially, psychoanalysis is not simply a body of knowledge to be brought to bear on that (more or less recalcitrant) object, cinema. Certainly, the fundamental concepts of psychoanalysis – sexuality, unconscious, fantasy, symptom – have been elaborated in a distinct body of work. Psychoanalysis can lay claim to a language and a domain of its own; Freud's thinking does do something to the meaning, and reach, of sexuality and dream, shock and trauma, in the twentieth century. Yet neither language nor domain stand alone. Psychoanalysis is intertextual, forged through a range of different disciplines and systems of thought which keep it open to the cultural objects it attempts to understand. Freud's writing is bound to the figures of drama and myth, for example. Oedipus, Narcissus, the uncanny: the language of literature, as Shoshana Felman points out, is the language through which psychoanalysis names itself, speaks about itself (Felman 1982: 9). Similarly, from the very end of the nineteenth century, a preoccupation with the power of the visual (image, hallucination) and the effects of fascination (hypnosis, identification) is shared between psychoanalysis and cinema – a sharing that begins to complicate the idea of psychoanalysis as a means to interpretation, a knowledge to be applied to cinema as an object from which it is distinct. (In fact, the very idea of application – from the Latin *applicare*: to join to, to fold together – is troubled by the concept of intertextuality.[4]) Psychoanalysis and cinema are already together, open to one another, in a way that psychoanalytic film theory is only just beginning to explore (what Anne Friedberg has described as the 'still unwritten and untheorized metahistory of psychoanalysis and cinema' (Friedberg 1990: 41)).

How to consider that history? Various approaches have been broached: studies in 'Freud at the Movies'[5] which draw attention to Freud's well-known mistrust of Hollywood; psychoanalysis as an object of interpretation by cinema (from G.W. Pabst's *Secrets of a Soul* (1926) – one of the first attempts to represent the process of a psychoanalytic cure on screen – to Alfred Hitchcock's *Spellbound* (1944));[6] the repeated coincidence between the topics of psychoanalysis and cinema. Stephen Heath's account of cinema as both alternative and successor to the nineteenth-century novel, for example, casts psychoanalysis as a discourse able to mediate the exchange between the two (Heath 1981: 125). Love, war, sexuality, family, death: these are the common themes of psychoanalysis and cinema, the ground upon which they meet (like, but not too like). The encounter between the two in psychoanalytic film theory is, as Robert Stam has put it recently, the 'culmination of a long flirtation' (Stam 2000: 159).

One of the aims of this book is to explore, and to explicate, the different models of mind and cinema which have contributed to the development of contemporary psychoanalytic film theory. That theory, it should be said, is both more and less than a theory of *film*. Preoccupied with the question of vision and image, sexuality and fantasy, wish and narrative, ideology and institutions, psychoanalytic film theory takes place in a diverse (sometimes dazzling) intellectual context. It is a context that has contributed to the notorious difficulty of some psychoanalytic writing on cinema – a difficulty that has directed the course of this book.[7] Psychoanalysis has been used to devise a conceptual grid through which to explore both how cinema works – the specific technology and language of film, its articulation of narrative and image, its appeal to a spectator caught up in the play of images on screen – and its privileged themes. Even a cursory reading of the (by now canonic) texts in psychoanalytic film theory shows a number of concepts which recur, gathering meaning across the domains of psychoanalysis and film. Hallucination, pleasure, wish, imaginary, hysteria, subject, spectator, apparatus, lack: the concepts emerge in disparate, and sometimes contradictory, ways through Freud, through his readers, marking the boundaries of the exchange between studies in psychoanalysis and film.

It can be a challenge to keep track. There are a number of invaluable introductions to the topic of psychoanalysis and cinema, as well as studies which use a range of psychoanalytic concepts to explore the work, and pleasures, of film and spectatorship.[8] This book does not attempt to re-cover that ground. Rather, focusing on a specific enquiry, each chapter attempts to make the field of psychoanalytic film theory *readable* by tracking its concepts back into psychoanalysis. I have said that cinema is a challenge to reading Freud, reading psychoanalysis. To push the point, if psychoanalytic film theory is to *enable* its readers, an introduction of this kind must encourage them to delve into the writings on which it (film theory) is drawing. Doing justice to Freud – reading psychoanalysis in context, as a body of work with its own questions and aims – is an important, but not the only, issue. If film theory is to avoid a reductive application of psychoanalytic concepts to cinema, then psychoanalysis must be read as a complex, diverse, and sometimes hesitant collection of writings. Both hesitancy and diversity may encourage confidence in new readers who have to start somewhere – with Freud, I think, if psychoanalytic film theory is to be read and questioned anew.

This introduction to the field has been written with that reading, and questioning, in mind. The book falls into two basic sections. Beginning with Freud's studies of hysteria in Paris in the mid-1880s, Chapters 1 and 2 work through the concepts of hallucination and hypnosis, wish and dream, at the origins of psychoanalysis – concepts that, from the mid-1970s, help to generate psychoanalytic film theory. Chapters 4 and

5 explore the founding myth of the Oedipus complex in Freud's thinking and its place in his controversial accounts of sexuality and sexual difference. Both myth and controversy have been central to the textual analysis of film pioneered by psychoanalytic film theorists (notably, Raymond Bellour) as well as the feminist challenge to those theorists which begins with Laura Mulvey's inaugural essay, 'Visual Pleasure and Narrative Cinema' in 1975. Each chapter focuses closely on a 'scene' between psychoanalysis and film theory (in the broad sense: theory of image, narrative, institution), on the questions and debates through which a psychoanalytic interpretation of cinema has found its purchase. It is a basic assumption of the book that close critical reading of key texts in both psychoanalysis and film theory is one of the most productive ways to clarify and to enliven both question and debate: crudely, to ground the abstract terms 'psychoanalysis' and 'film theory' in (more manageable) words on a page. I have tried to unpack the conceptual links that have been obscured at times, as well as to indicate how, and what, psychoanalysis helps us to think in contemporary film theory.

Chapter 3 bridges the two parts of the book with a discussion of a script which is now engaging the attention of film scholars and psychoanalysts alike: Jean-Paul Sartre's *The Freud Scenario* (edited by psychoanalyst, Jean-Bertrand Pontalis) was commissioned by the American director John Huston in 1958 but never filmed. As such, it is a remarkable reflection not only on the origins of psychoanalysis but on cinema as an institution which, as I hope to suggest, goes well beyond the flickering of images on screen.

1 FROM CHARCOT TO FREUD: THE ORIGINS OF PSYCHOANALYSIS

'Hallucination that is also a fact': this is André Bazin's stark analysis of the power of the cinematic image (Bazin 1967: 16). Early cinema lured its spectators with the promise of perceptual illusion, 'documents' of everyday life: the madding crowds of city streets, a family at dinner, workers leaving a factory. This is, as one commentator was to put it following the first demonstration of the Lumières' *Cinématographe* at the Grand Café, life 'collected and reproduced' (Burch 1990: 21). At the same time, as Maxim Gorky pushes to remind his readers, cinema is a haunted way of seeing the world. 'If you only knew how strange it is to be there,' Gorky writes in his troubled account of the 'kingdom of the shadows' in 1896. 'It is not life but its shadow, it is not motion but its soundless spectre' (Gorky, cited in Popple 1996: 97).

There is, it seems, something uncanny in the connivance of reality and illusion achieved by cinema, the impression made on its spectators. 'The spellbound audience in a theater or in a picture house' wrote Hugo Munsterberg in one of the first psychological analyses of film in 1916, 'is certainly in a state of heightened suggestibility and is ready to receive suggestions' (Munsterberg 1970: 47). As Lynne Kirby points out in her important discussion of Munsterberg, this association between cinema and suggestion, spectator and the subject of hypnotism, has a long tradition (Kirby 1997: 155). From the very beginning of cinema, the deluded – hysterical, traumatised, hallucinating – spectator is a source of comedy. In

Kirby's example, *Uncle Josh at the Moving Picture Show* – an Edison/Porter film from 1902 – 'parodies the Lumière spectator responding to the train' (65). Like Munsterberg's suggestible spectator, Uncle Josh is seduced into believing that it is 'life' he sees as the image of the train, *The Black Diamond Express*, rushes towards him. A figure of fun, perhaps, but Uncle Josh's panic – his (momentary) conviction in the present reality of the object on screen – confirms how far cinema was prepared to reflect on itself as an institution bound to exhibit the effects of suggestion: hallucination, false perception of an object which is 'not there'.

The question of how far the experience of cinema, the perception of the filmic image, can be compared to that of hallucination was central to the development of a psychoanalytic film theory in the 1970s. In this sense it is important to grasp what psychoanalysis does with the fact of hallucination, as well as the phenomena so often associated with it: hypnosis, suggestion. Like cinema, psychoanalysis is bound to the relation between the two: cinema and psychoanalysis share parallel histories (to borrow Janet Bergstrom's recent phrasing) which, at times, appear to converge (Bergstrom 1999: 1). The first half of this chapter explores one such scene of convergence: the origins of Freud's thinking in the spectacle of hysteria and hallucination on display at the Salpêtrière Hospital during his studies in Paris in the mid-1880s. It is a spectacle – of shock, of illusion – which has been compared to that of early cinema as both one of the distractions of fin-de-siècle Paris (the city of image and pleasure, as Vanessa Schwartz has argued) and a decisive moment in the visualisation of mental illness through the use of camera and photograph.[1] The second half of the chapter looks in some detail at Freud's early collaboration with his colleague and mentor, Josef Breuer. Part of the puzzle of the early history of psychoanalysis concerns the transition from Freud's studies with Charcot to his discovery (or invention) of the unconscious in the course of his treatment of a wide range of neurotic patients in Vienna in the closing years of the nineteenth century. In particular, Breuer's account of the case of Anna O., and Freud's response to it, can be used to bring into focus the difference of Freud's thinking about hallucination and memory, narrative and fantasy – the concepts through which Freud begins to elaborate psychoanalysis as a mode of interpretation which can be brought to bear on the experience, and objects, of modern culture.

The spectacle of hysteria

> A proper assessment and a better understanding of the disease only began with the works of Charcot and of the school of the Salpêtrière inspired by him. Up to that time hysteria had been the *bête noire* of medicine. The poor hysterics, who in earlier centuries had been burnt or exorcised, were only subjected, in recent, enlightened times, to the curse of ridicule. (Sigmund Freud, 'Hysteria' (1888))

> ... these symptoms have the body as their theatre. (Monique David-Ménard, *Hysteria from Freud to Lacan* (1989))

In the summer of 1885, the Faculty of Medicine at the University of Vienna awarded a travelling grant to the young Sigmund Freud ('by thirteen votes to eight', he wrote, jubilantly, to his fiancée, Martha Bernays, on 20 June that year (Freud 1992: 155)). Freud had applied for the grant with one aim in view: to study with the renowned Jean-Martin Charcot, Professor of Neuropathology at the Salpêtrière Hospital in Paris. 'In the distance,' Freud recalled, years later, in his 'Autobiographical Study', 'shone the great name of Charcot' – the man who, with some daring, was transforming medical understanding of the symptoms gathered under the term 'hysteria' (Freud 1925: 11).

Hysteria, 'the most enigmatic of all nervous diseases', as Freud calls it in his obituary for Charcot (Freud 1893: 19). As both disease and enigma, hysteria has a long history, one that can be traced back to the oldest sources of recorded medicine (the Egyptian *Kahun Papyrus*, from about 1900 BC, for example, deals with the manifestations of hysteria). Yet, as Ilza Veith points out in her fascinating study of the disease, hysteria 'defies definition', resisting and adapting itself to the diverse cultures in which it occurs (Veith 1965: 1). From the 'migratory womb' diagnosed by the ancient Greeks – 'Sorely disturbed, and straying about in the body,' writes Plato in *Timaeus* – to the chimera of sexuality and demonism common to the Middle Ages, to the battery of debilitation – paralysis, convulsion, vomiting – described by physicians through the nineteenth century, hysteria appears to mutate according to the concerns, and contradictions, of its culture (7, 120). At the same time, there is something enduring in the symptoms that have taken on its name. Notably, from the Greek *hystera* (womb), hysteria announces its privileged association with women and the disorders of female sexuality. It is an association, at once ancient and modern, which will become a powerful resource for both psychoanalysis and cinema.

When, in 1975, Hélène Cixous and Catherine Clément sketched an account of early cinema as part of the modern institutionalisation of hysteria, they pointed to the tangled relations among psychoanalysis, femininity and spectacle which are the subject of this chapter. In the 'expressive, expressionistic women of the silent films, their mouths open wide in unformulated cries', Cixous and Clément find an image of the women who helped Freud to bring psychoanalysis into being (Cixous and Clément 1986: 13). A cinema of silent women: seduced, seductive, suffering. That silence, its presentation as a pleasure and distress to be looked at, sustains this feminist analogy between cinema and the controversial psychology of hysteria emerging towards the end of the nineteenth century. As we will see, in his use of photography as a technique for visualising mental illness, Charcot has his place in the history of that institutionalisation of hysteria. Charcot and cinema share the camera: a passion for looking and recording what is seen. At the same time, the lack of an identifiable organic cause for the dramatic disturbances of the body taking place at the Salpêtrière Hospital points to the realm of (psycho)pathology that will captivate Freud: the work of mind and feeling in the production of the hysterical symptom.

Freud's trip to Paris was decisive. Arriving in the city in October 1885, he was immediately seduced by what he described as the 'plethora of new and interesting material' on display in Charcot's clinic (Freud 1886: 9). A hospital for women, the Salpêtrière housed some 5,000 patients; the 'dregs of society', as Veith calls them: 'neurotic indigents, epileptics, and insane patients, many of whom were deemed incurable' (Veith 1965: 236, 229). As senior physician, Charcot was in charge of the Department of Ordinary Epileptics, and immersed in the problems of hysteria. 'We are faced,' he noted, 'with a kind of *living pathological museum* of considerable resources' (Pontalis 1981: 20). Convulsions, paralyses, contractions, tics, hallucinations: the symptoms encountered by Charcot were often extraordinary, a wild theatre of bodies. With his background in pathological anatomy – the investigation of the body as clue to the understanding of disease – Charcot began to explore that theatre. The *arc en cercle*, for example, in which the body is 'bent in a bow-like curve and is supported only by the neck and the feet; the hair is dishevelled; the extremities are agitated by the clonic *"grands mouvements"* of flexion and extension and the mouth is opened widely' (Veith 1965: 231). An image of Bedlam, part of the chaos that confronted Charcot in his attempts to distinguish hysteria from other types of mental disorder suffered by the women of the Salpêtrière.

In so doing, Charcot was writing against a medical tradition which, as Freud was to point out in 1888, was in the habit of 'allotting the descriptions "hysteria" and "hysterical" capriciously, and of throwing "hysteria" into a heap along with general nervousness, neurasthenia, many psychotic states and many neuroses' (Freud 1888: 41-2). As the *bête noire* of the medical profession, hysteria was frequently ridiculed and dismissed, along with those who suffered from it. 'These patients are veritable actresses,' wrote Jean-Pierre Falret in 1866, expressing a keen repugnance for the disease. 'In one word, the life of the hysteric is nothing but one perpetual falsehood' (Veith 1965: 211). It was a prevalent view through the nineteenth century: the hysteric as malingerer, liar, deviant (a counter to that other Victorian image of the woman as an 'angel in the house'); hysteria as a 'false', or simulated, condition unworthy of serious attention.[2] Against this, Charcot – a man with a 'passion for careful observation and orderly classification' – began to build up his clinical picture of the disease (Bernheimer and Kahane 1985: 6). 'He used to look again and again at the things he did not understand,' Freud recalls in 1893, 'to deepen his impression of them day by day, till suddenly an understanding of them dawned on him' (Freud 1893: 12). But looking, and looking again, Charcot could discover no *organic* cause for what was happening to his patients: there was nothing 'wrong' with their bodies. At the same time, he insisted, whatever *was* wrong was real; hysteria was not simply a vicious plea for attention, its suffering was neither false nor feigned. The disease, he insisted, could also occur in men, a claim likely to arouse protest amongst some medical professionals. For Charcot, the symptoms of so-called 'railway brain' (a phenomenon observed in the (often male) victims of railway, and industrial, accidents) matched his own extensive description of hysteria and hysterical attacks. In particular, the *grande hystérie*, the pure type of hysteria, being observed at the Salpêtrière. 'An attack proper, if it is complete,' Freud summarised in 1888, 'manifests three phases':

> The first, "epileptoid", phase resembles a common epileptic fit. [...] The second phase, that of the *"grands mouvements"*, manifests movements of wide compass, such as what are known as "salaam" movements, arched attitudes (*arc de cercle*), contortions and so on. [...] The third, *hallucinatory*, phase of a hysterical attack, the *"attitudes passionnelles"*, is distinguished by attitudes and gestures which belong to scenes of passionate movement, which the patient hallucinates and often accompanies with the corresponding words. During the entire attack consciousness may either be retained or be lost – more often the latter. (Freud 1888: 43)

'Rare and strange material', Freud notes, reporting back to the University of Vienna in 1886: the age-old enigma of hysteria (Freud 1886: 6). But, as the psychoanalyst Jean-Bertrand Pontalis has pointed out, Charcot uses that material to open up a 'new space' – a space charged with the prehistory of both psychoanalysis and cinema (Pontalis 1981: 20). 'The stenographer is not a photographer,' Charcot wrote to Freud in 1891; that is, Freud's calm words cannot capture the visual shock of hysteria. His quiet reference to the resources available to Charcot at the Salpêtrière – among them, a 'studio for photography' – is no preparation for the impact of the spectacular record of hysteria that emerged from Charcot's teaching (Gelfand 1988: 571; Freud 1886: 7). Compiled between 1876 and 1878, for example, the remarkable *Iconographie photographique de la Salpêtrière* is the product of an alliance between psychiatry and photography: its succession of images give a body to clinical accounts of the convulsions and contractures – as well as the moments of stillness and ecstasy – experienced at the Salpêtrière. 'A roll-call for the phases and postures of the hysteric,' is how Pontalis describes it: 'the art of eroticism', a 'sexual topography that could easily serve as a set of instructions for perverts (front view, back view, it's all there!)' (Pontalis 1981: 21).

A strong statement, but one which bears witness to a certain excess of, and a felt investment in, the body of the woman in Charcot's vision of hysteria. There was a section designated for male hysterics at the Salpêtrière, but its *Iconographie photographique...* is a catalogue of women, variously posed: *Supplication, Extase, Erotisme, Tetanisme*. Images are staged, and staggered. As Stephen Heath points out in his discussion of these documents, there is a 'series of plates for a single patient, an attempt at duration, a movement in time'; an attempt, that is, to figure the space and time of the unfolding of a hysterical attack (Heath 1992: 52). Some of the women are photographed over and over again. 'The effect is of a kind of cinema,' Heath concludes, a response which echoes through the literatures on Charcot's imaging of the hysteric. 'Film *avant la lettre*,' proclaims Friedrich Kittler in the course of a brief discussion of Freud, Charcot and improvements in the speed of photographic processes from the late 1870s: 'Charcot's engineer Albert Londe, inventor of the Rolleiflex, had already in 1883 built a camera with nine or twelve lenses that took successive snap shots on the command of a metronome' (Kittler 1997: 94).

Cinema *avant la lettre*? The camera, as Kittler indicates, helps Charcot to *see* something: 'How beautiful and grand must the hysterical curve have turned out when cameras were able to store or produce it' (*ibid*.: 94). A new technology of vision enables an image of beauty, grandeur, eroticism and, perhaps, violation. The impact of *Iconographie photographique...* owes something to the intimacy, and intrusion, exercised by the camera closing in on women with tongues protruding, faces and neck in spasm. This is an obliteration of privacy that casts the hysteric in the role of grotesque (the other side of the eroticism emphasised by Pontalis). Again, it is an intrusion that finds a parallel in early cinema. Consider, for example, the 'experiment with the moving camera' described by Noël Burch in his brief commentary on *A Subject for the Rogues Gallery*, a Biograph film from 1904, in which three men force a woman (a prostitute) to pose for the camera:

> The prostitute tries to avert her gaze but the men force her to confront the oncoming camera; still struggling to *withhold her image* she contorts her features; but finally, in close-up, she breaks down and cries. (Burch 1990: 271)

It is an experiment which gestures towards the future of cinema as an institution, Burch suggests: 'the violation of the female face'. This early, and cogent, model of the film-spectator relation travels from the profilmic event to the image of looking on screen – a mix of voyeurism and sadism which psychoanalytic theory has made central to its analysis of the pleasures, and distresses, of cinema. In so doing, that theory is taking its cue from a cinema that continues to probe the acts, and scenes, of looking to which it is so closely bound. Think, for example, of Michael Powell's still controversial *Peeping Tom* (1960). The story of a young man who films the terrified faces of his (female) victims as he kills them, Powell's film seems both to confirm Burch's insight into the destination of cinema and to hark back to the surveillance of the female body which supports Charcot's studies in hysteria. The *transfer* of sadistic voyeurism from man to woman, from father to son (in *Peeping Tom*, the murderer has been traumatised by his father's intrusive surveillance) is one of the privileged themes of Powell's film – a theme in which a psychoanalysis of cinema can begin to find its purchase in a shared history, a shared preoccupation.[3]

Similarly, a sense of violation is never far away in contemporary accounts of Charcot's experiments at the Salpêtrière – notably, that aspect of his work which will bear most directly on Freud: hypnosis (a term which is going to travel between psychiatry, psychoanalysis and cinema). Faced with a disease which yields no sign of damage to the nervous system, Charcot turns to the study of hypnotism.

Hypnosis became a major diagnostic tool at the Salpêtrière, a means to distinguish between an 'organic' symptom and a hysterical one. Prepared to broach a subject that, as Freud puts it, 'had to be wrung on the one side from scepticism and on the other from fraud', Charcot discovered that the symptoms of hysteria could be reproduced by hypnotic suggestion: the compelling, commanding words of a 'master' (Freud 1886: 11). Hypnosis, he claimed, was a symptom of the illness – a claim that would add to the controversy of the Salpêtrière. Magnetisers drew large crowds in Paris through the 1880s, with performances on the cusp between healing and theatre.

Such performances were condemned by a medical establishment keen to distance itself from a tradition that, nevertheless, haunts Charcot's Clinic; in particular, the popular public lectures (the 'Tuesday Lessons') at which he explained, and exhibited, his female patients. 'Some of them smelt with delight a bottle of ammonia when told it was rose water,' recalls Axel Munthe, one member of the large audience of doctors, journalists, artists and authors attracted to Charcot's 'show'. 'Another would crawl on all fours on the floor, barking furiously when told she was a dog, flap her arms as if trying to fly when turned into a pigeon' (Munthe, cited in Showalter 1987: 148).

Pierre André Brouillet's lithograph of Charcot lecturing at the Salpêtrière offers another view on this scene of hysteria and hallucination: the 'Master', Charcot, facing his audience; between Charcot and his assistant, the female patient – supposed to be Blanche Wittman, 'Queen of the Hysterics' – exposed, back arched, apparently in the throes of an attack; the spectators (all male) ranged on the other side of the room and, behind them, an illustration of the dreadful *arc en cercle*. 'The circularity of the scene is perfect,' notes Pontalis in his brief commentary on the painting, 'all the characters, even the footlights – the light projected through the high windows – are in the appropriate place' (Pontalis 1981: 21).

In years to come, Brouillet's famous image will hang above Freud's equally famous couch, a constant reminder of where psychoanalysis begins. It is easy to imagine Freud in that eager front row, leaning forward, captivated as much by Charcot's presence as by the 'cases' on display. 'My brain is sated as after an evening in the theatre,' he writes to Martha Bernays on 24 November 1885, reflecting on the experience of working with Charcot. 'No other human being has ever affected me in the same way' (Freud 1992: 185). It is a powerful statement of Charcot's influence on Freud, his ability to captivate his listeners – 'spellbound by the narrator's artistry no less than by the observer's penetration', as Freud recalls (Freud 1892-94: 135). Casting a spell over his audience, binding it to him through the pleasures of spectacle and story, Charcot plays a key role in Freud's early ideas on hysteria: that is, in the very origins of psychoanalysis. What Freud sees and hears at the Salpêtrière turns him towards the study of psychology, the invisible world behind the phantasmagoria of symptoms. Not that Charcot himself, Freud tells us, was interested in that world, in what his patients said or felt. He looked, he described, he classified, but 'took no special interest in penetrating more deeply into the psychology of the neuroses' (Freud 1925: 14). 'You see how hysterics shout; much ado about nothing' is his much-quoted phrase (Heath 1992: 53).

Back in Vienna, struggling to establish his practice as a specialist in nervous disorders, Freud begins to transform his experience of looking with Charcot into the speaking and listening of psychoanalysis. Essential to that work of transformation is Freud's approach to the hysterical body, his way of working through the problem that dominates Charcot's Clinic: the distinction between hysterical and organic symptoms. That distinction was to become the subject of one of Freud's most important early papers, 'Some Points in a Comparative Study of Organic and Hysterical Paralyses', described by his editors as the 'watershed between Freud's neurological and psychological writings' (Freud 1888-93: 158). Acknowledging his debt to Charcot and the Salpêtrière at the very beginning of the essay, Freud goes on to sketch a proto-psychoanalytic account of what he had encountered in Paris. Hysteria, he argues, betrays itself in (at least) two ways. First, it behaves as though anatomy does not exist. A hysterical paralysis of the arm, for example, will conform not to the distribution of nerves along the limb but to the patient's *idea*, or *image*, of her arm. Hysteria, Freud continues, 'takes the organs in the ordinary, popular sense of the names they bear: the leg is the leg as far up as its insertion into the hip, the arm is the upper limb as it is visible under the clothing' (169). Not a medical but a popular idea of the body – imaginary, fantasmatic – governs the formation of a hysterical symptom. The hysterical body, Freud suggests, is derived from 'our tactile and above all our visual perceptions' (70).

What we can touch and see come right to the fore in hysteria, then, this tactile and visual disorder through which a body is forged; a body (if that is what it is) composed of, and *so subject to*, images, words and ideas. It will become part of Freud's life work to understand this body: first, its response to the authority and voice of the hypnotist; later, the connection between life – what his patients can, and cannot, tell him about their lives – and symptom. From this point of view, the invention of psychoanalysis coincides with a shift from image to speech: 'Charcot sees, Freud hears' is Stephen Heath's bold summary of the change that supports psychoanalysis as a new theory, and therapy, of mind (Heath 1992: 53). Or, less dramatically perhaps, psychoanalysis is one way to think about how spectacle is bound to language and narrative (one of the questions that will be shared with studies in cinema); that is, how the image of her body which animates the hysteric is bound to her ways of being, and experiencing, the world.

To put this another way: while Charcot demonstrates the hysteric's willingness to see, touch, smell, an object which 'isn't there' – going so far as to reproduce his patients' hallucinations under hypnosis – Freud will attempt to discover the meaning behind his patients' symptoms, to restore a link between the spectacle of hysteria and the thoughts and feelings which support it. Not to reproduce the symptom, then, but to interpret it; not to look, and look again, but to listen for the story – wishful, anxious, traumatic – embedded in the image.

The Fictions of Anna O.

> The principal technical innovation of psychoanalysis was the removal
> of the therapist from the hysteric's field of vision, so that she was
> forced to make herself heard and was no longer before a real spec-
> tator in whose eyes she might find the desire that she sought. (René
> Major, 'The Revolution of Hysteria' (1974))

> Jorge Dana asked me once if it could really be an accident that the
> cinema began just as Freud was abandoning hypnosis and initiating
> a technique of *blind dialogue*. (Noël Burch, *Life to those Shadows*
> (1990))

One case stands out in the history of Freud's shift of attention from reproduction to interpretation, spectacle to story: the case of Anna O. Treated
by Breuer, between 1880 and 1882, Anna O. (or Bertha Pappenheim, to
give her real name) has become known as the 'first patient' of psychoanalysis, the woman credited with inventing that well-known phrase, the
'talking cure'. Freud always maintained that psychoanalysis was discovered by Breuer, that the first psychoanalysis was Breuer's treatment of
Anna O. Not a view, it should be said, with which Breuer would concur.
Nevertheless, what Breuer had told him of this young woman would have
stayed with Freud during his studies in Paris – a kind of setting for Charcot's theatre of hysteria and, later, the tensions of Freud's own practice.
It is a setting through which Freud is able to discover the foundations of
psychoanalysis in the relation between speech and cure, as well as the
unique tie between therapist and patient. At the same time, the attention
to fiction – to daydreaming and hallucination – in Breuer's accounts of
his treatment of Anna O. will help Freud towards a new understanding of
the importance of his patients' wishes. 'All our stories,' as Adam Phillips
has put it recently, 'are about what happens to our wishes' (Phillips 1998:
1). It is this way of thinking about the work of wishing in illness and creativity which marks the difference of psychoanalysis – its approach to a

patient's distress, certainly, but also to the work of culture. The concept of the wish, the understanding of fantasy and fiction to which it gives rise, supports a psychoanalytic study of culture. Crucially, as an institution driven by the wish – a mode of 'public fantasy', as Elizabeth Cowie has put it – the fiction of cinema lends itself to psychoanalysis, to a psycho-analytic reading of the vicissitudes of wishing embedded in the narratives and images of film (Adams and Cowie 1990). But what, precisely, is a wish for Freud? What does psychoanalysis do (or not do) to the idea of fiction? How do we begin to describe a wish on screen, in film? Such questions take us back to the origins of psychoanalysis.

First diagnosed by Breuer as hysteric towards the end of 1880, Anna O. endured a set of debilitating, sometimes terrifying, symptoms. 'While she was nursing her father,' Breuer writes in his published account of the case in 1895, 'she had seen him with a death's head' (Freud and Breuer 1895: 37). On another occasion, falling into a 'waking dream', again at her father's bedside, the patient 'saw a black snake coming towards the sick man from the wall to bite him' (38). Paralysis, somnambulism, hallucina-tion, loss of speech, alternating states of consciousness: Anna O.'s symp-toms were baffling, but not uncommon. What singles her out in the his-tory of hysteria is the process of her treatment, the 'chance observation' which puts Freud and Breuer on the track of a fundamental link between speech and cure (3). 'The patient fell into a somnolent state every after-noon,' Breuer explains his case, 'and after sunset this period passed into a deeper sleep – "clouds"' (28). Watching his patient closely, Breuer notices how, becoming increasingly restless in her sleep, she begins to repeat the words 'tormenting, tormenting'. 'It was also noticed,' he continues,

> how, during her *absences* in day-time, she was obviously creating some situation or episode to which she gave a clue with a few muttered words. It happened then – to begin with accidentally but later intentionally – that someone near her repeated one of these phrases of hers while she was complaining about the 'tormenting'. She at once joined in and began to paint some situation or tell some

> story. [...] As a rule their starting-point or central situation was of a girl anxiously sitting by a sick-bed. [...] A few moments after she had finished her narrative she would wake up, obviously calmed down, or, as she called it *'gehäglich'*. (28-9)

Intimate, complex, controversially erotic, Breuer's relationship with Anna O. changed the nature of the contract between doctor and patient.[4] It is clear that Breuer devoted himself to this treatment. Hour upon hour was spent in listening to what she said under her 'clouds': the English word was Anna O.'s term for the state of absence – a 'deep hypnosis', a *condition seconde* – which was interrupting her experience of daily life (32). In Breuer's view, there were two distinct states of consciousness present in his patient: the one, depressed and anxious but relatively normal; the other, hallucinatory, disruptive and subject to bizarre distortions of time and place. In the second year of her illness (1881-82), for example, Anna O. began to relive the winter of 1880-81. She experienced her past life with such intensity that, as Breuer records, she 'hallucinated her old room', knocking up against objects around her, unable to find her way to the door and window (33).

Whatever this state is, then, it is characterised by a powerful fictionality: *fiction* in at least two senses. On the one hand, her 'second state' is dominated by Anna O.'s experience of an image which carries an overwhelming impression of reality; fiction is bound to the image, to the special role played by the visual in the self's experience of a world as 'real', as 'really there'. For Breuer and for Freud (as for the spectators of the Lumières' *cinématographe*), the lure of the image is able to trouble the distinction between reality and hallucination. Seeing things which are not there, Anna O. screens out the world in which others are living; she is able to sustain what Breuer diagnoses as a 'negative hallucination' (27). She refuses to be 'present' with (literally, refuses to *see*) who, or what, she does not wish to see: doctors, family members, unwelcome guests.

On the other hand, the act of making up stories is fundamental to the drama enacted between Anna O. and Breuer who is struck by his patient's tendency to live in a dream-world, to daydream her way through the boredom of her daily existence. 'Bubbling over with intellectual vitality,' he notes, '[she] led an extremely monotonous existence in her puritanically-minded family' – another description which flies in the face of that contemporary view of the hysteric as degenerate (22). By contrast, on Breuer's account his patient's hysteria is inseparable from the banality of her family life, the limitations imposed upon her as a woman in late nineteenth-century Vienna.[5] Anna O. is described as 'markedly intelligent', her 'penetrating intuition' and 'great poetic and imaginative gifts' combine with energy and sympathetic kindness towards others even at the height of her illness (21). But her round of household duties – and, later, her exhausting role as nurse to her dying father – is stultifying and distressing. Her way out is daydreaming, and then illness: the link between the two is part of the interest of Anna O.'s case. 'She embellished her life,' Breuer explains, 'in a manner which probably influenced her decisively in the direction of her illness, by indulging in systematic day-dreaming which she described as her "private theatre"' (22). Dramatic and wishful, her theatre is Anna O.'s way to find, and represent, the satisfaction that would be otherwise missing from her life. Those around her could not tell what she was doing – 'she was always on the spot when spoken to' – but Anna O. was continuously 'living through fairy tales in her imagination', telling herself stories, playing her part in a series of internal dramas the content of which we can only guess. In her case, Breuer was convinced, the habit of daydreaming had passed over imperceptibly into hysteria – as if the spectacular symptoms of hysteria can come to embody the intimacy of the daydream. What links the two is that bizarre state of being 'in the clouds', where consciousness is lulled and distracted – hypnotised – into a scene able to make its existence more tolerable.

It is tempting to view Anna O. as a prototype of the bored and frustrated, exhausted and wishful, spectators so often supposed by commentators on that other form of systematic daydreaming: cinema.[6] Anna O.'s passage from daydreaming to hallucination, from 'private theatre' to hysteria, is imperceptible – stages on a continuum sustained by the power of her wishes to find condensed, and distorted, expression in story and symptom. 'We may lay it down,' Freud writes in the course of a discussion of the creative writer and daydreaming, 'that a happy person never phantasies, only an unsatisfied one' (Freud 1908: 146). This is not a view that psychoanalysis will sustain, but it does draw attention to Freud's insight into how what we wish for becomes embroiled with what we imagine and represent to others, to ourselves, through our symptoms and our stories. In other words, the wish is tied to the domain of representation in a way that will open to the door to a psychoanalytic interpretation of the meaning of narratives and images. The idea of a wish, struggling to find expression – in distorted, even bizarre form – will become one of the basic assumptions of psychoanalytic interpretations of cinema, its role in the anxieties, and pleasures, of everyday life.[7]

At the beginning of the 1880s, however, Breuer's primary concern is with the possibility that Anna O.'s suffering can be relieved by the act of talking to him. Listening closely to his patient's muttering, Breuer uses her own words to cue her, encouraging Anna O. to express her torment in fictional form, to create the 'poetical compositions' that bring some relief to her agitated state of mind (Freud and Breuer 1895: 29). In other words, the disturbance of Anna O.'s illness gives way before the plot and pattern of her narrative (as if part of the work of aesthetic imagination is to make bearable the chaos of having a mind). As her illness deteriorates, so Anna O.'s hallucinations take on a life of their own, displacing her fictions. 'Her evening narratives,' Breuer recalls, 'ceased to have the character of more or less freely-created poetical compositions and changed into a string of frightful and terrifying hallucinations' (29). Such a distinction between hallucination and poetry may well be crucial to a psychoanalytic account of creativity – with the speech of psychoanalysis, putting self states into words, somewhere between the two. A type of catharsis – a purging of tension and feeling – is how Freud and Breuer describe it, drawing on a term that, like psychoanalysis itself, rests on the cusp between literature and medicine. Consider, for example, the following key passage from their 'Preliminary Communication', published in 1893:

> For we found, to our great surprise at first, that each individual hysterical symptom immediately and permanently disappeared when

we had succeeded in bringing clearly to light the memory of the event by which it was provoked and in arousing its accompanying affect, and when the patient had described that event in the greatest possible detail and had put the affect into words. Recollection without affect almost invariably produces no result. (6)

The implications of this tie between memory, speech and cure are far-reaching. Anna O.'s symptoms are 'talked away' through words which appear to have the power to heal the distortions of the hysterical body. That is, what Anna O. helps Freud and Breuer to discover is the link between talking and recovery, the tie between symptom and memory. 'Hysterics suffer mainly from reminiscences' is their well-known conclusion, as if hysteria (like the camera) can be understood as a technique of memory (7). Unable to remember whatever it is that she cannot forget, the hysteric suffers from a form of division of consciousness. A memory has been 'cut off', *dissociated* from consciousness. Left to its own devices, such a memory will forge associations with other ideas excluded from the conscious mind, laying the foundations for what Freud and Breuer describe as the 'more or less highly organised rudiment of a second consciousness' (15). It is that second consciousness (Freud's first glimpse of the unconscious) which is supposed to emerge under hypnosis, when the patient's consciousness is no longer there to thrust it away. Anna O.'s stories and reports come through in this second state, her 'clouds', in which she is able to give some account of her bodily and visual disturbances. Taking each symptom separately, Breuer talks his patient back through to the situation in which that symptom makes its first appearance. A strenuous but effective process. 'When this had been described,' he writes, with apparent confidence, 'the symptom was permanently removed' (35).

On this reading, the aim of psychoanalytic therapy is to restore to the hysteric a narrative which has gone missing from the mind, to restore a series of links which have been attacked and broken. What motivates such an attack remains a troubling question for Freud: shock, pain, distress – including the distress of disappointed, or unwanted, wishes – can all contribute to the turning away which, opening up a gap in consciousness, leaves the hysteric bewildered.[8] Note the difference from Charcot: the hysteric is not a woman susceptible to hypnosis but a woman unable to tell a story. Narrative, not hypnotism, is the preferred tool of diagnosis; the hysterical symptom comes in the place of a story which cannot be told. Hysteria fills in the gaps in language and narrative with body and hallucination – as if the symptom becomes the depository of something that the mind is striving to forget.

What Freud and Breuer were coming up against in hysteria, then, was a division of consciousness that, as Freud puts it, 'must greatly facilitate the occurrence of "false connections"'; the wish to thrust away, or repress, what is in some way shocking or distressing to the mind opens up a gap, a rift (Freud and Breuer 1895: 67). In these circumstances, Freud concludes, we are likely to 'invent a story', or a symptom, to find a way to account for what we think and feel and do. In other words, there is a type of compulsion to fill up the gaps in consciousness that psychoanalysis discovers first in the context of hysteria, but which Freud will soon describe as a normal process of the mind as such: repression, an attempt to repel that which the self cannot bear to know. It is Freud's innovation to turn that repression into a therapeutic, and critical, resource. Frustrated at his own lack of success with hypnotism, Freud will develop new techniques: first, the 'pressure technique' in which a gentle pressure on the patient's forehead is used to urge her to have confidence that she can, and will, recall whatever it is that she claims not to remember; then, the basic principle of psychoanalysis: free association, in which the patient is asked to say whatever comes into her head. In any case, there is, as Freud quickly discovers, a 'special solicitude' inherent in analytic treatment: the emotions of both analyst and patient are engaged in, and acted upon by, what happens between them in a unique way (Freud and Breuer 1895: 302). The memories and wishes, thoughts and feelings, lived through the speech of psychoanalysis become attached to the figure of the analyst, the time and setting of psychoanalysis itself. How the patient uses the analyst, how she actualizes her wishes and conflicts in the analytic situation, will become one of the privileged objects of psychoanalytic attention. Towards the end of his own contribution to *Studies on Hysteria*, in fact, Freud will describe that situation as a type of illusion, a *transference* onto the analyst of ideas and feelings which belong to other times, other places, and other people in the patient's history. 'Transference on to the physician,' he notes, acknowledging the discomfort this so often involves for the patient, 'takes place through a *false connection*' (302).[9] False connection and invented story: the work of transference binds the theory, and practice, of psychoanalysis to the world of fiction.

Through the 1880s and 1890s, Freud continued to refine his theory of the relation between wish and symptom, fantasy and the division of consciousness. 'I have gained a sure inkling of the structure of hysteria,' he writes to his then friend and colleague, Wilhelm Fliess, on 2 May 1897. 'Everything goes back to the reproduction of scenes. Some can be obtained directly, others always by way of fantasies set up in front of them' (cited in Masson 1985: 239). This is one of Freud's first uses of what will become a major (and mutable) concept in psychoanalysis and psychoanalytic approaches to film: fantasy. 'Fantasies are psychic façades,' he continues to Fliess, 'produced in order to bar access to these memories'; like neurotic symptoms, they are 'protective structures', 'protective fictions', defending against, by trying to elaborate the experience of, the trauma which calls them into being.[10] Barring access to memory, for example, fantasy appears as a form of defence against a reality felt to be unbearable. That is, Freud's understanding of fantasy entails a reference to *pain* which immediately complicates a familiar association between wish(fulfilment) and pleasure. A wish does not always aim at pleasure.[11] Fictions, daydreams, are conjured by a subject who feels the need for protection. Fantasy intervenes. It comes between the self and its history, consciousness and reality – making use of things seen, heard, and experienced to rework the world. Fantasies, Freud concludes, 'combine things experienced and heard, past events (from the history of parents and ancestors), and things that have been seen by oneself' (240).

There is, it seems, no limit to the reach of fantasy, its role in our attempts to contain the trauma, as well as the banality, of our lives. Fantasy elaborates – proliferates, disguises, distorts – around a kernel of 'reality' that quickly becomes the vanishing point of Freud's theory.

Symptom and 'scene' become so entangled with one another that the task of talking each one back to its point of origin (Breuer's account of his procedure with Anna O.) is hopeless. It is impossible – for Freud, for his patients – to bring any case to rest. Instead, as he announces to Fliess on 21 September 1897, there is the hallucinatory reality of the unconscious – a place (a state?) in which 'there are no indications of reality ... so that one cannot distinguish between truth and fiction that has been cathected with affect' (264). It is a moment of indecision in which Freud begins to wonder how what his patients are saying to him relates to their personal history. What are his patients talking about? Memories? Wishes? A peculiar confabulation of the two?[12] What are they reliving – dramatically, perhaps cathartically – in the intimate space of Freud's consulting-room? Remember that therapeutic adage: 'Recollection without affect almost invariably produces no result.'

Freud is doing more than simply listening to his patients. He observes. He is witness to the emotions, and gestures, which accompany their (sometimes terrible) stories: typically, of the sexual violence of family life.[13] Was this another type of 'private theatre', to borrow Anna O.'s phrase? Cinema *avant la lettre*? Certainly, part of what Freud has to account for is the vivid realism of his patients' narratives, whatever it is that is driving them to relive a scene that may never have happened. Is this an effect of the unconscious? And if so, what is it? A profoundly wishful, and fictional, place, is Freud's first (and provisional) response to that question: an 'other scene' where one cannot distinguish between truth and fiction that has been cathected with affect. That is, so far as the unconscious is concerned, wishes do come true; fiction can be real. But what are these wishes, and where do they come from?

Such questions take Freud into his monumental study of *The Interpretation of Dreams*, its powerful exploration of the wishes, at once sexual and murderous, supposed to preoccupy us all. Wishes that, Freud tells us, are to be found not only in our dreams but also in the formations of social, political and cultural life. As we will see in discussion of the 'typical' fantasies – of self, of sexuality, of difference – trafficked through Hollywood cinema (Chapters 4 and 5), part of the wager of psychoanalytic film theory has been to identify the work of those wishes in film. For now, though, let us stay with Freud's struggle to find a way to talk about his new ideas on memory, sexuality and fantasy (in particular, the hallucinatory reality of the unconscious). It is a struggle that he pursues via the dream – 'the royal road to a knowledge of the unconscious activities of the mind' (Freud 1900: 608) – and which lends to psychoanalytic film theory one of its founding metaphors: the analogy between cinema and dreaming.

2   THROUGH THE LOOKING-GLASS:
   MIRROR/DREAM/SCREEN

In fact, the moment at which screen division starts to operate coincides with the first appearance of the mirror in segment four, at this
point still containing Baldwin's image. For the first time, Baldwin
faces his reflection, here in a mock duel, specifically as an opponent ('My opponent is my mirror image'). (Leon Hunt, *Der Student
von Prag*)

If the cinema is not made to translate dreams or all that which, in
conscious life, resembles dreams, then the cinema does not exist.
(Antonin Artaud, *'Sorcellerie et cinéma'* (1927))

A parallel between dream and cinema had often been noticed:
common sense perceived it right away. The cinematographic
projection is reminiscent of dream, would appear to be a kind
of dream, really a dream, a parallelism often noticed by the
dreamer when, about to describe his dream, he is compelled to
say, 'It was like in a movie ...'. (Jean-Louis Baudry, 'The Apparatus:
Metapsychological Approaches to the Impression of Reality in
Cinema' (1992))

In 1914, a compelling scene opens up between psychoanalysis and
cinema. 'Not long ago,' wrote Otto Rank at the very beginning of his

psychoanalytic study of *The Double*, 'a romantic drama made the rounds of our cinemas' (Rank 1971: 3). Rank is referring to a strange and powerful film made for Bioscope by Stellan Rye and Hanns Heinz Ewers in 1913: *Der Student von Prag* (*The Student of Prague*). One of the first films to bring the Romantic and psychoanalytic theme of 'the double' – a reflection, a double consciousness – to the screen, *Der Student von Prag* tells the story of an impoverished scholar, Balduin, who loses his mirror image to a sorcerer in exchange for wealth and fame. Lured out of the mirror, Balduin's reflection takes on a life of its own, tormenting the student and, finally, driving him to suicide: the shot he fires at the apparition of his double kills Balduin.

'It was a brilliant film idea,' concludes Siegfried Kracauer in 1947, drawing attention to a correspondence between cinema – what it is, what it can do – and the idea of the double: a man pursued by himself (Kracauer 1947: 29). Rye's use of the split, or divided, screen to achieve the Doppelgänger effect is one way to solve what Willy Haas has described as the 'film problem of all film problems': the doubling of the actor to perfection (cited in Kittler 1997: 96). Rank, too, is interested in what cinema is going to do with this Romantic, and literary, theme. Reminding his readers of Ewers' debt to the fiction of E.T.A. Hoffman and Edgar Allan Poe – that is, of cinema's debt to Romantic and Gothic literature – Rank is also keen to speculate on cinema's capacity to represent both mind and dream. 'It may perhaps turn out,' he muses, tantalisingly, 'that cinematography, which in numerous ways reminds us of the dream-work, can also express certain psychological facts and relationships – which the writer often is unable to describe with verbal clarity – in such clear and conspicuous imagery that it facilitates our understanding of them' (Rank 1971: 4).

The idea of cinema as a new technique of vision able to make the processes of the mind – imagination, dream, 'psychology' – more apparent, runs through early psychoanalytic responses to film. In fact, via a brief footnote on Rank's book, *Der Student von Prag* even makes its way into Freud's influential essay, 'The Uncanny', first published in 1919 – one of the few glimpses of cinema between the lines of his work. Freud's own lack of interest in cinema is legendary. 'FREUD REBUFFS GOLDWYN: Viennese Psychoanalyst Is Not Interested In Motion Picture Offer': the headline which ran in *The New York Times* on 24 January 1925 announced Freud's lifelong suspicion of cinema. According to his biographers, Freud – the 'greatest love specialist in the world', as Goldwyn described him to a journalist from the paper – had declined an offer of $100,000 to advise on a 'really great love story' (Gay 1988: 454; Jones 1957). In a one-line telegram that caused uproar in New York, Freud refused to see Goldwyn, shying psychoanalysis away from an apparently unwelcome association with Hollywood. Similarly, in 1926, he resisted attempts to involve him in the production of *Secrets of a Soul*, a film directed by Weimar luminary G.W. Pabst. 'I do not believe,' Freud insisted to his colleague, Karl Abraham, 'that satisfactory plastic representation of our abstractions is at all possible' (cited in Friedberg 1990: 44).[1]

Nevertheless, the brief encounter between Rank, Ewers and Freud anticipates two key themes in the film theory of the 1970s. On the one hand, the analogy between screen and mirror – the idea of the self founded in, and opposed by, its reflection in a mirror, on screen – sustains Christian Metz's discussion of cinema as a 'strange mirror', the spectator as a type of 'double of his double' before the image on screen (Metz 1982: 4). Drawing on the work of one of the most influential figures in modern French thought, the psychoanalyst Jacques Lacan, Metz shifted the ground of studies in psychoanalysis and cinema – a shift which, currently disputed by Lacanian scholars of film, is the point of focus for the second half of this chapter.

On the other hand, both Metz and Jean-Louis Baudry were engaged with the comparison between cinema and dream – a comparison so pervasive that, as Baudry was to put it in 1975, there is a 'common sense' slippage between the two. It is a theme that echoes through writing on psychoanalysis and cinema. 'The analogy of dreaming with the filmgoing experience,' writes Toby Miller in his introduction to one of the most comprehensive recent anthologies, *Film and Theory*, 'is obvious – no surprise that Hollywood's newest studio is "Dreamworks"' (Stam and Miller 2000: 477).

Starting from Freud's radical reworking of the idea of dream and dreaming as a form of hallucinatory wish fulfilment, this chapter explores the web of connections between these two themes. In the first instance, what does it mean to compare cinema to dream? Is the connection so apparent? After all, what could be more intimate, more singular, than a dream? It is a question that, as Harvie Ferguson points out in *The Lure of Dreams*, derives from a very modern understanding of the dream as 'subjective, irrational and illusory' (Ferguson 1996: 1). The idea of the dreamer as a being withdrawn from the world, of the dream as the creation of a world apart, has a history – a history to which, in the course of the twentieth century, both cinema and psychoanalysis make their contributions. 'Freud,' Ferguson suggests, 'opened out the dream once again and, so to speak, spread it across the surface of waking life' – a description that could equally be applied to cinema (159). That is, both psychoanalysis and cinema change the idea of the dream in modern cultural life. Grounded in Freud's model of a psyche driven by wish and hallucination, it is part of the wager of psychoanalytic film theory to describe that change – the collusion, and coincidence, between dream and cinema as 'techniques' of the imaginary.

'Thoughts transformed into images'

> I want to reveal to you only that the dream schema is capable
> of the most general application, that the key to hysteria as well
> really lies in dreams. (Freud to Wilhelm Fliess, 4 January 1899)

The idea of the dream as a world full of meaning, thought and work, runs through *The Interpretation of Dreams* – the book which, as Freud was to put it in 1931, 'surprised the world when it was published'. That surprise has something to do with Freud's claims for the significance of dreams, their reach into the domains of illness and creativity. 'Anyone who has failed to explain the origin of dream-images,' he insists, 'can scarcely hope to understand phobias, obsessions or delusions or to bring a therapeutic influence to bear on them' (xxiii). That is, there is a link between dreaming and madness, dream and cure: if you want to understand the meaning of symptoms, you have to understand both *what*, and *how*, dreams mean. At the same time, Freud explores the obscure, often ingenious, work of dreams through the dramas of literature and creativity. Sophocles' tragedy of *Oedipus Rex* will give its name to the basic complex of psychoanalysis (the Oedipus complex) while Freud is keen to cast the psychoanalyst as a man of science forced to behave like a poet. 'If I was to report my own dreams,' he explains in the first preface to the dream-book in 1900, 'it inevitably followed that I should have to reveal to the public gaze more of the intimacies of my mental life than I liked, or than is normally necessary for any writer who is a man of science and not a poet' (xxiii-xxiv).

On the cusp between medicine and literature, psychoanalysis invests itself in the scientific (Freud will stress this word) interpretation of dreams – an interpretation that, we now know, formed part of Freud's own self-analysis, his development of the techniques of psychoanalytic therapy (Anzieu 1986). But what, precisely, is the common thread connecting therapy to dream, creativity to symptom? What does Freud find in dreams that prompts him to describe them as the key to the problem of the psychoneuroses? The wish and the child, in fact: the wishes of the child living on in the dreamer. 'No one even suspects,' Freud writes to Fliess on 16 May 1897, 'that the dream is not nonsense but wish fulfilment' (Masson 1985: 243). That insight drives Freud's thinking through *The Interpretation of Dreams*; the idea of the wish at the origins of the self – 'Nothing but a wish can set our mental apparatus at work,' Freud maintains – is one of the foundations of his discovery, the psychoanalytic account of self and representation on which film theory draws (Freud 1900: 567). Crucially, it is a wish which belongs to a child; the child that the dreamer once was (and still is): 'We find the child, and the child's impulses,' Freud insists, 'still living on in the dream' (589)

It is in this sense that Freud's understanding of dreams and dream life is bound to his theory of infancy and childhood, of fantasy and sexuality. At the heart of *The Interpretation of Dreams* is an infant: screaming and helpless, driven by a desire for satisfaction. Let us call it 'The Story of the Hungry Baby' – a tale which is finally told towards the end of the dream-book in Freud's lengthy chapter on 'The Psychology of the Dream-Processes'. In the course of one of his concluding discussions of wish fulfilment in dreams, Freud sketches the following scenario:

A hungry baby screams or kicks helplessly. But the situation remains unaltered, for the excitation arising from an internal need is not due to a force producing a *momentary* impact but to one which is in continuous operation. A change can only come about if in some way or other (in the case of the baby, through outside help) an "experience of satisfaction" can be achieved which puts an end to the internal stimulus. An essential component of this experience of satisfaction is a particular perception (that of nourishment, in our example) the mnemic image of which remains associated thenceforward with the memory trace of the excitation produced by the need. As a result of the link that has thus been established, next time this need arises a psychical impulse will at once emerge which will seek to re-cathect the mnemic image of the perception and to re-evoke the perception itself, that is to say, to re-establish the situation of the original satisfaction. An impulse of this kind is what we call a wish; the reappearance of the perception is the fulfilment of the wish; and the shortest path to the fulfilment of the wish is a path leading direct from the excitation produced by the need to a complete cathexis of the perception. Nothing prevents us from assuming that there was a primitive state of the psychical apparatus in which this path was actually traversed, that is, in which wishing ended in hallucination. (565-6)

Freud's striking account of the origin of wishing will run throughout the various literatures of psychoanalysis. Helplessness, *Hilflosigkeit*, is his key word: a state of being which is going to determine the baby's relation to herself as well as to those around her. Defenceless in the face of her every need, the baby depends on someone (or something) from the outside to help her to suck, to feed, to sleep, to play. The fact of being helpless, in other words, is going to turn her towards the world, towards the helpers who may (or may not) hear her scream or, later, her call. In this sense, the baby's helplessness is profoundly socialising, the very origin of her compulsion towards community and culture. But it also founds a way of being, and relating, to herself which is decisive to Freud's understanding of the dream. Agitated but powerless, Freud's baby turns in on herself, opens up an internal space for the mind, in her attempts to conjure up the *memory of a previous experience of satisfaction*. Freud is very careful on this point. Baby and wish are aiming not, or not only, at the pleasurable sensations of satisfaction but at the mental *image* – the mnemic image, in Freud's terms – of that satisfaction ('an impulse of this kind is what we call a wish'). In its drive to pacify her, the wish opens up the space of memory and representation for the baby (and, it should be said, for psychoanalysis). An imaginary scene of satisfaction – a fantasy, precisely – comes to displace, however temporarily, the unbearable pressure of her needs. It is a moment of illusion, of magical control, that psychoanalysis will go on to describe as essential to the development of mind and creativity.[2]

Let us note that, once again, Freud is exploring the idea of wish and fantasy in terms of the self's attempts to transform the experience of pain. The hallucinatory wishing of infancy is the product of the baby's attempt to help herself – a form of protection as well as pleasure. Wishing herself into and out of the world, the baby is the model of the fantasising subject for Freud; she is at the very core of missing and wanting to be discovered in us all. Especially in our dreams. Hallucination, hallucinatory reproduction of the mental image, is the shortest route to pleasure. And the baby takes it, over and over again. 'The first wishing,' Freud explains, 'seems to have been a hallucinatory cathecting of the memory of satisfaction' (598). That is, the wish always harks back to hallucination – a primary hallucination that, for Freud, can begin to explain the dream's tie to the visual, the image. A form of identity between perception and memory, hallucination is the mind's first attempt at wishing, and it exerts a permanent pull on the subject – in dreams, certainly, in visions, but also in what Freud

describes as our 'pathological waking states': notably, the deliria of paranoia and hysteria (544). (Put this way, there is a risk to the pleasures of
image and hallucination: the risk, finally, of illness or death. What would
be the effect of an hallucination that could not be exhausted: a question
for the new technologies of virtual reality, perhaps?) Hallucination is also
one of the sources of that vivid realism of the unconscious on which
Freud comments to Fliess: there are no 'indications of reality' in the
unconscious; as in our dreams, its wishes (and nightmares) do come true
(Masson 1985: 264).

In many ways, *The Interpretation of Dreams* works back from this story
to describe, and defend, its basic thesis of the dream as a form of wish
fulfilment. What Freud is discovering in infantile life is a form of mental
functioning that he will describe as primary and unconscious. Bypassing
the tests of reality and reason, the primary process is governed by a
different logic in its handling of ideas, words, images. Above all, it is characterised by a drive to 'pleasure', the urgent fulfilment of a wish, derived
from infantile life. The dream, Freud maintains, is a 'substitute for an
infantile scene modified by being transferred on to a recent experience'
(Freud 1900: 546). Freud has his sights on both the wish (sex and aggression will be the privileged themes) and the work: hallucination (the means
to its achievement). The mechanisms of the primary process involved
in the production of the dream, he tells us, have a pronounced prefer-
ence for ideas and feelings which can be represented in visual form.
Moving over the mass of the dream-thoughts and wishes, the dream-work
(one of Freud's terms for the mechanisms of the primary process) is both
creative and defensive. It modifies – more strongly, disguises – the
infantile wishes which have prompted the dream by condensing them,
scrambling them, into the frequently bewildering experience of dreaming.
'A dream is a (disguised) fulfilment of a (suppressed or repressed) wish':
in Freud's renowned definition, the wish – disguised, distorted, worked
on – lies buried in the dream, a message waiting to be recovered through
the labour of dream interpretation (160).

Even in the dream, it seems, the child's wish cannot speak its name.
Instead it is forced to reside in what Freud describes as the latent content

of the dream. By contrast, the manifest dream appears to the dreamer: a 'narrative in images', as Laplanche and Pontalis describe it, and one which may well be distressing and unwished for (Laplanche and Pontalis 1973: 235). But why the disguise? Freud ponders the question throughout *The Interpretation of Dreams*. Some dreams, Freud acknowledges, are open forms of wishfulfilment. But, he continues, 'in cases where the wish fulfilment is unrecognisable, where it has been disguised, there must have existed some inclination to put up a defence against the wish' (Freud 1900: 141). It is a vision of the mind in a state of continuous, and interminable, conflict with itself – a struggle between wish and defence, wish and censorship, wish and repression. (Very much like a city-state, Freud suggests, in one of the founding metaphors of psychoanalysis (142).) With the power of authority on its side, the censor blocks the passage of the wish from unconscious to conscious; that is, censorship represents the law, the wish its transgression. But the censor is also at the disposal of the wish, creating the façade that will enable it to break through into the conscious mind, to make its presence known. In other words, censorship works towards a compromise between law and desire, conscious and unconscious (with dream, like the symptom, as one of its effects).

It would be difficult to overestimate the influence of Freud's idea of the dream as a 'text', a type of hieroglyph, forged through the compromise between two forces. Breaking the dream down into its (often-disconnected) elements of images, words, and phrases, Freud read across the manifest content to discover another narrative embedded in the dream – a narrative closely bound to the dreamer's wishes and fears. In other words, psychoanalysis is invented as a theory of reading in which a wishful-shameful text is found running alongside – more precisely, perhaps, in between the gaps of – another. One scene – object, wish, anxiety – is substituted, and so comes to stand, for another. It is an approach to reading which opens up the manifest content of a text – be it dream, film, or literature – to the voice(s) of desire and anxiety concealed by, and finding expression through, it. One scene glimpsed in terms of another, and then another, until, more likely than not, the psychoanalyst-reader comes up against the unfathomable tangle of words and thoughts which, as Freud states and restates in *The Interpretation of Dreams*, is the very 'navel' of the dream, 'its point of contact with the unknown' (111).

It may be that repression is given an essential maternal dimension in Freud's use of the figure of the navel to describe the effects of distortion and displacement on the possibility of (and necessity for) reading as such. Certainly, Barbara Creed's *The Monstrous-Feminine: film, feminism and psychoanalysis* – one of the most influential uses of psychoanalytic reading in film theory – begins with the question of how the figure of the mother makes itself felt through the science and horror fictions of popular cinema (Creed 1989: 73).[3] In her extensive commentaries on Ridley Scott's *Alien* (1979), for example, Creed explores both the absence of the mother on screen ('the "mother" as a figure does not appear in these sequences', she notes in the course of her reading of the opening scenes of the film (75)) and what she describes as the 'image of the mother in her generative function' – the phantasm that supports the visual and narrative world of the film (73).

Absorbed by processes of birth and impregnation, the monstrous 'something' which attaches itself to the face of its victims, *Alien* is driven by an exorbitant desire to *know* – the secrets of the cavernous ship, cast in the shape of vagina-uterus, in which Kane insists on pursuing the enigma of the alien life-forms – and the trauma unleashed by that pursuit: oral penetration, the implantation of the alien in its (human) host, the threat to the lives of the crew of the *Nostromo*. The perverse 'birth' – the alien exploding from Kane's chest – is one of the canonic scenes of modern horror film, a displacement of the scene of birth from woman/mother to man, from vagina-womb to mouth-chest. It is a displacement which, on Creed's reading, disguises the pervasive presence of the mother in the film, her role as a 'vast backdrop for the enactment of all events' (75). Displacement, too, that draws attention to the oral anxiety which so marks Scott's film. Think, for example, of the attempt on Ripley's life by Ash (the android science officer), the effort to kill her by thrusting a rolled magazine down her throat. Such a moment of excess (is this the most rational way to kill?) opens up its images, and narratives, onto another scene – an anxiety, flickering between and behind what we see on screen.

Certainly, the idea of a hidden, or secret, story waiting to be recovered cuts across Freud's understanding of both symptom and dream. In Chapter 4, we will come back to what, for Freud, remains one of the key secrets embedded in dreams: the story of Oedipus, a type of navel for both psychoanalysis and film theory in their joint pursuit of the elusive relation between wish, censor and dream. In the remainder of this chapter, we stay with that hallucinating baby – the baby who puts Freud on the track of an unconscious bound to pleasure and image, an unconscious which finds expression through the illusory, and animated, world of the dream. 'Here we have the most general and the most striking psychological characteristic of the process of dreaming,' Freud concludes in the course of his discussion of the impression of reality in dreams: 'a thought, and as a rule a thought of something that is wished, is objectified in the dream, is represented as a scene, or as it seems to us, is experienced' (534).

In other words, what the dream-image represents for Freud is confirmation that a normal capacity for hallucination persists in us all. From the mid-1970s, it is that idea of normal hallucination, together with its counterpart – the baby playing with, fantasising through, the image – which will be imported into the psychoanalytic study of film to produce an account of cinema as, in Jean-Louis Baudry's phrase, a 'simulation apparatus': a technology directed to the hallucinatory reproduction of the real through the figure of a spectator captivated by the image on screen (Baudry 1992: 702).

Dream/apparatus

Actually, cinema is a simulation apparatus. This much was immediately recognised, but, from the positivist viewpoint of scientific rationality which was predominant at the time of its invention, the interest was directed toward the simulation of reality inherent to the moving image with the unexpected effects which could be derived from it, without finding it necessary to examine the fact that the cinematographic apparatus was initially directed toward the subject and that *simulation could be applied to states or subject effects before being directed toward the reproduction of the real.* (Jean-Louis Baudry, 'The Apparatus' (1975))

From the beginning of the 1970s, the dialogue between cinema and psychoanalysis returns to the question of dream and dreaming to develop a theory of cinema as what, in his decisive contributions, Jean-Louis Baudry describes as an 'apparatus'. It is worth pausing on this word because it opens up onto a number of different, but related, topics in psychoanalytic film theory. In particular, the idea of apparatus announces a preoccupation with the technology of cinema, its specific use of camera, screen, projection, movement, image. All the elements that, as Tom Gunning has shown, moved the earliest audiences of cinema to astonishment: cinema as a machine, a new technology of vision (Gunning 1997). At the same time, the concept of apparatus is used to invoke what Christian Metz identifies as the 'mental machinery' which comes to meet cinema, the institution 'outside us and inside us', as he puts it at the beginning of his groundbreaking study, 'The Imaginary Signifier', (Metz 1982: 5).

From technology to spectator, from institution to psyche: the body of work collected under the term 'apparatus theory' is one of the most sophisticated reflections we have on representation in cinema; more precisely, on that juncture between cinema and world known as the subject or spectator. 'So you see,' writes Baudry, 'we return to the real or, for the experiencing subject (I could say, for the subject who is felt or who is acted), the impression of reality' (Baudry 1992: 691). Baudry's phrasing is decisive: the 'impression of reality' is the initial point of contact between cinema and dream, cinema and subject. That is, apparatus theory inherited, and reworked, discussions of representation and realism (discussions which quickly come up against the topic of aesthetics and politics: the cinematic naturalisation of 'things as they are' is one of the key charges against cinema as source of resistance to social change).[4] In cinema, Baudry clarifies, that impression 'is different from the usual impression which we receive from reality, but which has precisely this characteristic of being more than real which we have detected in dream' (702). In the dream, that *more-than-real* is derived from a number of features which will be used to support the analogy between cinema and dream. On Baudry's reading:

> The transformations accomplished by sleep in the psychical appa-
> ratus: withdrawal of cathexis, instability of the different systems,
> return to narcissism, loss of motoricity (because of the impossi-
> bility of applying the reality test), contribute to produce features
> which are specific to dream: its capacity for figuration, translation of
> thought into images, reality extended to representations. One might
> even add that we are dealing with a *more-than-real* in order to dif-
> ferentiate it from the impression of the real which reality produces
> in the normal waking situation: the more-than-real translating the
> cohesion of the subject in his representations, the near impossibil-
> ity for him to escape their influence and which is dissimilar if not
> incompatible with the impression resulting from any direct relation
> to reality. (700)

This is a difficult passage (one that, it should be said, carries the 'flavour' of much of the prose associated with psychoanalytic film theory). Diffi-cult, in part, because 'The Apparatus', like Baudry's earlier essay, 'Ideo-logical Effects of the Basic Cinematographic Apparatus' is working out from a reading of psychoanalysis: Freud, certainly, but also, as we shall see, Jacques Lacan's influential 'Return to Freud'. In particular, his profile of the subject as one on whom reality is going to be (has to be?) *impressed* is indebted to Freud's exploration of the dreamer as wishful and hallu-cinating. Reality, it seems, is not simply there to be discovered; it has to make itself felt, the subject has to test it out, test for it – part of the long, and painful, process through which we learn to tell the difference between what we perceive and what we imagine.[5] In dream, in fantasy, in cinema, it is a difference that can be put under pressure. Baudry, like Metz, will attempt to specify those features of the dream that, reflected in the experience of cinema, contribute to its impression of reality: the spectator's withdrawal from the world; her state of immobile, usually silent, reverie (in between waking and dream); the perceptual illusion so characteristic of narrative cinema (Metz 1982: 101-37). Not that there is a simple coincidence between cinema and dream. Rather, as Metz suggests, the 'gap between the two states sometimes tends to diminish'; cinema can become the 'delusion of a man awake', film can enter into 'functional competition with the daydream' (101; 109; 136).

To say this is to suggest that, like the dream, cinema depends in part on the spectator's capacity for 'normal' hallucination. As an industry bound to the reproduction of pleasure and image (of pleasure *through* the image), cinema draws on – or, 'reactivates' to borrow Metz's phrase – the hallucinatory scene that Freud discovers at the origin of the dream. It is in this sense that both Baudry and Metz will attempt to track the connections between the impression of reality in cinema and Freud's conception of the primary process as a visual order driven by the wish. Narrative cinema, Metz insists in a brief note on the images of 'satiety and fulfilment' trafficked through Hollywood film, 'is always to some extent regressive': that is, the function of the image in Hollywood cinema is to encourage a type of backward movement through the mind from the modes of thinking characteristic of the secondary processes (attention, judgement, reasoning) to the hallucinatory pleasures of the primary process (to want is to see is to have/experience) (92). As Freud points out, such a regression can be a normal aspect of waking life – part of the work of memory and recollection, for example (Freud 1900: 543). But it does not usually involve what he goes on to describe as the 'hallucinatory revival of the perceptual images', the revival proper to dream, to hallucination, to delusion.

And, on this reading, to cinema. 'The difficulties met by the theoreticians of cinema in their attempt to account for the impression of reality,' Baudry insists, 'are proportionate to the persisting resistance to really recognising the unconscious' (Baudry 1992: 703). Or, the fictional reality of cinema depends for its effect on the unconscious forms of mental work at the very origin of the psyche. To push the point, the unconscious is the condition of cinema, essential to the very act of watching a film. The wager of apparatus theory is its pursuit of the perceptual, and illusory, quality of cinema in two directions at once. On the one hand, in what Metz describes as the 'primary imaginary of photography and phonography': the material, the stuff, of cinema which combines techniques of vision and sound characterised by the production of perceptual illusion (Metz 1982: 44). That is, as Metz puts it, photograph and phonograph conjure the impression of image and speech *as* present in their absence. On the other hand, it is their attention to the *activity* of perception, to the subject doing the perceiving, which characterises the analyses put forward by Baudry and Metz. Through the comparison between film and dream, apparatus theory will introduce the question of the spectator into the psychoanalysis of cinema. For Baudry, that question can be used to counter what he presents as a history of film limited by its focus on the 'reality inherent to the moving image', by its neglect of the spectator who comes to receive that image:

> The key to the impression of reality has been sought in the structuring of image and movement, in complete ignorance of the fact that the impression of reality is dependent first of all on a subject effect and that it might be necessary to examine the position of the subject facing the image in order to determine the raison d'être for the cinema effect. (Baudry 1992: 702-3)

On the cusp between psychoanalysis, philosophy and cinema, Baudry turns film theory towards the relation between subject and image, subject and reality – a relation that he begins to describe in terms of *effects* (the subject as a type of 'special effect' of cinema). At issue, Baudry insists, is the 'subject effect', its relation to the 'cinema effect'; that is, the impression of reality on a subject brought into being by its look at the image on screen (702). But what is this 'subject'? This 'effect'? The concepts circulate, sometimes obscurely, through a film theory which grounds itself in psychoanalysis. Clearly, Baudry is using the figure of a society devoted to spectacle: the subject, facing the image, engrossed, absorbed, consuming. Put this way, it is clear that the analysis of cinema as an apparatus is prompted by a felt need to understand its force – at once, psychological and political, aesthetic and cultural. The exploration of the cinematic apparatus is a means to its critique as an institution of modern culture, as an ideological system which promotes the dominant (liberal, bourgeois) organisation of social life.[6] At the beginning of 'The Imaginary Signifier', for example, Metz's brief reference to Howard Hawks' *Red River* (1948) as a 'justification of private property and the right of conquest ... a misogynist variant of male homosexuality' suggests the frame of reference (Metz 1982: 30). Similarly, Baudry's analyses of cinema aim at its role as 'support and instrument of ideology': the ideologies through which we live our relation to the world ('Western history', 'capital', 'bourgeois hegemony': Baudry's terms do not lend themselves to precise navigation). Nevertheless, in its very attention to the question of who, or what, is the subject of cinema – *how* that subject is brought into being through the effect of cinema – both Baudry and Metz tend to displace the problem of the articulation between that subject and its cultural context: the question of why the dream/fiction of cinema takes one form rather than another (a question which returns in the feminist critique of apparatus theory discussed in Chapter 5).

At the same time, the exchange between subject and image, spectator and apparatus, in Baudry's analysis as well as Metz's exploration of the cinema as a 'technique of the imaginary' comes via one of the most influential essays in contemporary film theory: Jacques Lacan's 'The Mirror Stage as Formative of the Function of the I', presented at the International Congress of Psychoanalysis in 1949. Lending to film studies an account of the origin of subjectivity in the image – precisely, Baudry's subject-spectator *facing* the image – this essay has also been central to the various analogies between screen and mirror which have helped to generate psychoanalytic film theory. 'Film theory introduced the subject into its study,' Joan Copjec concludes in 'The Orthopsychic Subject', 'and thereby incorporated Lacanian psychoanalysis (Copjec 2000: 447). In fact, the predominance of the mirror stage, and Lacan's concept of the imaginary, in apparatus theory is now subject to some dispute within Lacanian film studies – a dispute which, turning on a close, and sophisticated, rereading of Lacan's theory of the gaze, tends to displace the concerns of apparatus theory. In this context, and given the notorious difficulty of Lacan's writing, it is worth going back to this inaugural essay to uncover the dynamic of image and identity that has held film theory in thrall. Once again, it is the story of a baby: 'The Story of the Baby and the Looking-Glass' which, before it reaches film theory in the 1970s, has a complex history of its own.

Through the Looking Glass

'I cannot urge you too strongly to a meditation on optics': in 1954, Jacques Lacan's advice to the students following his seminar for the *Société Française de Psychanalyse* bears witness to the centrality of apparatus and image in his thinking. 'The topic of the imaginary' was the subject of this seminar, an extended reflection on a concept which had been with Lacan since the 1930s: the mirror stage. Lacan borrows the term from psychologist Henri Wallon, a fact that, as Elisabeth Roudinesco points out in her fascinating intellectual biography of Lacan, he constantly plays down:

> An account of his different definitions of it reads like a serial story. He spoke passionately of it on about a dozen occasions, and when he published his *Ecrits* (Writings) in 1966 he emphasised again that the term had always been the pivot on which the development of his thought system turned. (Roudinesco 1997: 110).

The first instalment of that story comes in 1936 when, at the 14th International Congress of Psychoanalysis held in Marienbad at the beginning of August, Lacan delivered his contribution on the 'Mirror Stage'. Or rather, he tried to. Ten minutes into his presentation Ernest Jones who, as president of the London Psychoanalytic Society was presiding over the Congress, interrupted Lacan mid-sentence.

The following day, apparently rankled by that interruption, Lacan left Marienbad for the Berlin Olympiad, the eleventh Olympic Games that the Nazi ceremonials would turn into a spectacle of racist, and totalitarian, identifications.

Lacan did not send his paper for inclusion in the published proceedings of the Marienbad Congress. That first version, framed by controversy within the psychoanalytic institution as well as the growing Nazi threat, is lost. In 1949, the version so prominent in film theory, 'The mirror stage as formative of the function of the I as revealed in psychoanalytic experience', was delivered to the first post-war Congress of Psychoanalysis; nearly two decades later, it was included in Lacan's *Ecrits* (its importance is recognised in the English selection of *Ecrits* published in 1977 which opens with 'The mirror stage'). The essay can be (has been) read from a number of different perspectives: Lacan's attack on American ego psychology; his offensive against Cartesian philosophy; his critique of the ego as a delusive formation of modern culture; his discontent with the state of psychoanalysis as a theory, a practice and an institution that has lost sight of what is new, and radical, in Freud's thinking; and, in film theory, his attention to a subject bound in its very origins to the pleasures, and risks, of identification with an image.

Both pleasure and risk are explored through the captivating scene in which a baby is transfixed, jubilant before his own image in the mirror. We have to imagine Lacan looking on, fascinated by a spectacle of fascination. 'There may be some among you,' Lacan begins, addressing his audience with a veiled reference to Henri Wallon:

who remember the aspect of behaviour, clarified by a fact of comparative psychology, from which we began: the child – at an age when he is for a short time, but still for a time, surpassed in instrumental intelligence by the chimpanzee – is yet already able to recognise his image as such in the mirror. [...] That act, far from exhausting itself as in the case of the monkey, once the image has been mastered and found inane, is immediately revived in/by the child in a series of gestures by which he playfully tests the relation of the movements assumed in the image to his reflected environment and of this virtual complex to the reality it redoubles – to the child's own body and to people, indeed to things, around him. Since Baldwin, we know that this event can be produced from the age of six

.months, and its repetition has often arrested my attention before the startling spectacle of the nursling in front of the mirror, who has not yet mastered the art of walking, even of standing up, but who, held as he is by some human, or artificial, support (what we call in France a *trotte-bébé*) surmounts, in a jubilatory activity, the fetters of his supports in order to suspend his bearing in a more or less leaning position, and brings back, to fix it, an instantaneous aspect of the image. (Lacan 1977: 1-2, translation slightly modified)

Pulling faces, leaning forwards, struggling against whoever, or whatever, is supporting him, the baby gazes – as if trying to take a photograph of himself.[7] What is this baby doing? Being human, Lacan insists. That is, his comparison between the baby and the young chimpanzee (a little later, there are quasi-comic references to pigeons and locusts), suggests that what is at stake for Lacan is the difference of being human, the work, and play, involved in assuming a human identity as such. It is an identity, an 'I', which has to be *formed*, precipitated from the inchoate being of a subject 'still sunk in his motor incapacity and nursling dependence' (2). In this sense, what Lacan describes as a 'specific prematurity of birth in man' has real consequences for the baby who enters into the mirror stage in a state of helplessness – dependent for survival, and meaning, on the goodwill of others. The baby, looking into the mirror, is chaotic, insufficient, turbulent; by contrast, the image is a 'total form', an *image* of what might be, which thrusts the infant-spectator into a state of anticipation: the mirror stage, Lacan insists, is 'a drama whose internal thrust is precipitated from insufficiency to anticipation' (4).

What is beginning to emerge here is Lacan's influential theory of identity as a fantasy, a myth. 'This image is a fiction,' Jacqueline Rose explains in an Introduction to Lacan's psychoanalysis of subjectivity, 'because it conceals, or freezes, the infant's lack of motor co-ordination and the fragmentation of its drives' (Rose 1986: 53). In other words, the image is both spectacle and fabrication (a forerunner of fiction, of narrative), while the 'I' which emerges from the mirror stage is a confabulation of both. The drama of the mirror stage, as Lacan explains it, moves the subject from a 'fragmented body-image to a form of its totality that I shall call orthopae-dic' (Lacan 1977: 4). What the mirror does for the baby, caught up in the lure (Lacan's term) of his own reflection, is to hold out a promise. A fiction, a mirage, a *Gestalt*, an imago, an ideal: these are the terms in which Lacan describes that promise, the form in the mirror with which the baby is going to *identify*:

> We have only to understand the mirror stage as an identification, in the full sense that analysis gives to the term: namely, the transfor-mation that takes place in the subject when he assumes an image. [...] This jubilant assumption of his specular image by the child at the *infans* stage, still sunk in his motor incapacity and nursling depend-ence, would seem to exhibit in an exemplary situation the symbolic matrix in which the *I* is precipitated in a primordial form, before it is objectified in the dialectic of identification with the other, and before language restores to it, in the universal, its function as sub-ject. [...] But the important point is that this form situates the agency of the ego, before its social determination, in a fictional direction, which will always remain irreducible for the individual alone. (2)

The exchange between image and identity, image and identification, in this passage has been enormously productive for film theory. Transformed by the way in which she takes on (identifies with, precisely) the image reflected back to her from the mirror, the baby undergoes a type of pri-mordial structuring: the formation of an 'I' through which she begins to enter into a relationship with her own image, a relation which *precedes* the more familiar opposition between 'I' and 'you'. In fact, projecting her-self into her own image, the baby is preparing the ground for her relations with both self and others. That first identification, Lacan maintains, is also the 'source of secondary identifications' through which the subject is going to take up her, or his, place in the symbolic life of culture (as a son or a daughter, for example, man or woman, heterosexual or homosexual: the 'functions of libidinal normalisation' as Lacan puts it) (2). No mirror, no identity: Lacan will stress the point. It is the human baby who, on catching sight of her image in the mirror, is lured into the joyful fictions of her self as coherent, recognisable, *there*.

But, and decisively, she is also fractured in two. The image which grants the baby an imaginary coherence divides her twice over: (1) from the image in the mirror: the identity which is forged through the mirror stage comes from the outside, is external to the subject who identifies with it; (2) from the inchoate subject she was prior to that look in the glass. Reflecting on the consequences of such divisions, Lacan will turn to the topic of aggression – the alienation and paranoia that, he suggests, is the other side of the jubilant captivation which distinguishes the mirror stage. It is a perspective derived, in part, from Freud who, in his study of the structure of the ego in 1921, had discovered both love and aggression in the idealising process of identification. 'Identification, in fact,' he notes, in 'Group Psychology and the Analysis of the Ego', 'is ambivalent from the very first; it can turn into an expression of tenderness as easily as into a wish for someone's removal' (Freud 1921: 105). Keeping his eye on the baby in front of the mirror, Lacan tracks the various causes, and forms, of its love and aggression towards the image. The concluding passages of 'The Mirror Stage' present a condensed (one might say scrambled) history of the experience of subjectivity in modern culture.[8] At once isolated and rivalrous, fragile and fortified, the characteristics of the modern subject are read out of the dynamics of the mirror stage in which the image can become (1) a double, the object of attack (dangerous rival to the self it helps to found); (2) an ideal, an object to be defended (in the ego's attempt to maintain the image of what is loveable in the self, in others, Lacan will identify a certain inertia, a tendency to servitude); (3) an ideal but one subject to attack (unattainable, the image unleashes aggression); (4) an opponent, again the object of attack that, in 'Aggressivity in Psychoanalysis', Lacan had described as 'spring[ing] from the very bipolar structure of all subjectivity' (Lacan 1977: 10). That is, aggressivity describes a relation between the self and its image: the subject's identification with the ideal coherence of the image in the mirror is shadowed by a drive to violate that image, the very identity it brings into being. This is a splitting of the subject against itself which runs parallel with the split between baby and mirror. 'Intended aggressivity,' Lacan continues, 'gnaws away, undermines, disintegrates; it castrates; it leads to death' (10).

It is the source, too, of those unsettling images of the body – fragmented, persecuted, in pieces – which form part of the visual history of European culture. In 'The Mirror Stage', Lacan's privileged example is the 'visionary' Hieronymus Bosch whose paintings make the subject's attack against itself apparent 'in the form of disjointed limbs, or of those organs represented in exoscopy, growing wings and taking up arms for intestinal persecutions' (4). But this is a tradition of attack against the body inherited, and strenuously upheld, by cinema – from its early fascination with the railway accident to the spectacular evisceration associated with the modern horror genre in which, as Carol Clover points out, the 'opened body' takes centre stage (Clover 1989: 103; Kirby 1997). In this sense, cinema is one place to look for what Lacan describes as the *imagos* (of one's own body, of others) which make themselves felt through, and continue to structure, the reality of everyday experience. It is a powerful argument for cinema as a visual record of the forces of idealisation and aggression aimed at the human body – forces worked through a relation to the image which may be a source of pleasure, compensation or attack.[9] In fact the vicissitudes of the image in the mirror, on screen, become central to film theory through the 1970s and 1980s and, in particular, to the debates generated by Metz's founding analogy between screen and mirror – his turn to Lacan for an account of that *'other mirror*, the cinema screen' (Metz 1982: 4).

Ego/cinema: technique of the imaginary?

> A strange mirror, then, very like that of childhood, and very different. (Christian Metz, 'The Imaginary Signifier')

From *Der Student von Prag* to David Fincher's *Fight Club* (1999), cinema announces its preoccupation with the idea of the double, the risks of an *alter ego* (prop or opponent?). With the publication of 'The Imaginary Signifier' in 1975, the idea of the mirror and the (perilous) double coincide in film and film theory. From the beginning, Metz formulates the question which guides his study of psychoanalysis and cinema: What does the voyeurism of the spectator in cinema have to do with the primordial experience of the mirror? It is a question which acknowledges Metz's debt to Lacan's imaginary, to his psychoanalysis of subjectivity and fiction (the subject as a form of fiction) which is going to support a compelling account of cinema as a 'technique of the imaginary'. 'What is characteristic of the cinema,' Metz insists, 'is not the imaginary that it may happen to represent, it is the imaginary that it is from the start' (44).

It is a decisive moment in contemporary film studies when, as Constance Penley points out, Metz 'shifts the grounds of all previous discussions of the processes of identification in film' (Penley 1989: 12). On the one hand, cinema is imaginary in the common sense of the term. 'Most films consist of fictional narratives,' Metz notes at the beginning of 'The Imaginary Signifier'; or, in the rhetoric of Saussurean linguistics which runs through this writing, narrative film works with, and through, a 'fictional signified' (Metz 1982: 44). On the other hand, cinema depends on that 'primary imaginary of photography and phonography' described by Metz; cinema is both more and less perceptual than comparable art forms (literature, theatre, painting, musical performance). Cinema gives us the 'really perceived detail' of the world, 'all the animation of the street', that so captivated its early audiences (Méliès, cited in Gunning 1997: 119). The perfect illusion of the double – the actor beside himself – is one of the first triumphs of cinema, the mark of its difference from the illusory world of theatre.

But compared to a theatrical performance, say, the perceptual object of cinema is also uniquely absent. 'The activity of perception which it involves is real,' Metz clarifies his point, 'but the perceived is not really the object, it is its shade, its phantom, its double, its *replica* in a new kind of mirror' (Metz 1982: 45).

It is through this appeal to the metaphor of the mirror that Metz is able to designate the cinema screen as the domain of an 'other scene', its unfolding between presence and absence bringing it 'closer to phantasy from the outset' (43). (Compare Creed's comment on *Alien*: the image of the mother may be absent from the screen but she is nevertheless present in the film (Creed 1989).) 'What unfolds there [on screen],' Metz continues, 'may be more or less fictional, but the unfolding itself is fictive (43). It follows that there can be no simple act of perception in cinema. The visual is always more than (because less than) the perceptual: a 'more but less' that, for Metz, defines the cinematic world as fiction and illusion. 'Present in the mode of absence' is his suggestive phrase which, harking back to the play of insufficiency and anticipation that marks Lacan's description of the mirror stage, forms the conceptual bridge to Metz's identification between mirror and screen: 'Thus film is like the mirror' (45).

Prepared for throughout the opening chapters of 'The Imaginary Signifier', Metz's founding analogy arrives quite suddenly in his text, orienting his discussion of spectatorship and identification. Present/absent: the alternation between the two defines this mirror, Lacan's mirror, in which the baby, misrecognising the sufficiency of its reflection, identifies with the image of a being who is not (yet) there. But there is, Metz concludes, one essential difference. The spectator's body never appears in the mirror of cinema; his or her image is 'missing' from the screen. In other words, the identification which takes place in cinema is *not* that of the 'true' (Metz's word) mirror stage.

The spectator does not identify with his or her own image but with the act of perceiving the image as such – an act which is only possible, Metz suggests, because we have already looked at, and been in, the mirror. (Again, the act of looking in cinema is only possible in this account because the subject has undergone the primordial founding, and splitting, of the mirror stage; like the unconscious, the mirror stage is a condition of cinema). 'The spectator identifies with himself, with himself as a pure act of perception,' Metz concludes – an identification, finally, with the camera which sees all, which comes before the world it appropriates and constructs (49).

Part of the challenge of 'The Imaginary Signifier' for film theory is its insistence on the totalising, quasi-hallucinatory pleasures of that identification (one supposed to make possible the secondary identifications with image, with narrative). Metz's spectator, as Penley points out, is 'centred for absolute mastery over the visual domain'; the subject of film theory, Joan Copjec confirms, 'takes the image as a full and sufficient representation of itself and its world' (Penley 1989: 63; Copjec 2000: 441). What matters here is that the spectator mistakes the image for his, or her, *own* (not, or not only, in the sense of recognising him or herself in the image on screen, but in accepting that image as his or her image of someone/ something else). Certainly, this is the general drift of Metz's (and Baudry's) analysis: cinema as a type of lure to the ego, a 'psychical substitute', as Metz puts it, 'a prosthesis for our primally dislocated limbs' (Metz 1982: 4). It is a dislocation which puts us back in, or at, Lacan's mirror. But, as various critics have pointed out, by keeping the emphasis on cinema as a visual aid to the spectator's mastery, apparatus theory tends to lose sight of the paranoia and aggression that, for Lacan, will always accompany that fantasy of mastery.[10] It is a problem to which Metz gestures in his opening commentary on the imaginary as the 'durable mark of the mirror which alienates man in his own reflection and makes him the double of his double' (Metz 1982: 4). But 'The Imaginary Signifier' could only begin to explore the different scenarios implied by this insight. The idea of man as the 'double of his double' – the double who can always take on the form of persecutor – gives way before Metz's exploration of the pleasure principle at the heart of cinema: the desire, the passion for seeing, that keeps the machine going.

It will fall to other critics to take up different aspects of the machine, to rediscover the aggression and anxiety there, and waiting, on the other side of the mirror. The passion for seeing – the voyeurism and fetishism supporting that passion – will be engaged by feminist critics pursued by the image of woman in cinema (see Chapter 5). More recently, the 'return to Lacan' now taking place through the work of the Slovenian thinker, Slavoj Žižek, has challenged the dominance of the concept of the imaginary in film theory. In one of the most comprehensive anthologies of *Film and Theory*, the most recent contribution is Joan Copjec's powerful critique of film theory's use of Lacan's concept of the imaginary, 'The Orthopsychic Subject: Film Theory and the Reception of Lacan', first published in *October* in 1989 (Stam and Miller 2000). So far as film theory's use of Lacan is concerned, Copjec's essay indicates the shift of focus which has taken place between the 1970s and the 1990s. There is, on Copjec's view, a basic misconception at the heart of contemporary film theory:

> Believing itself to be following Lacan, it conceives the screen as mirror; in doing so, however, it operates in ignorance of, and at the expense of, Lacan's more radical insight, whereby the mirror is conceived as screen. (Copjec 2000: 437)

Tracing that misconception through Metz, Baudry and Jean-Louis Comolli as well as various feminist essays on film, Copjec goes on to suggest that, by insisting on the subject of cinema as one who misrecognises itself as 'source and centre of the represented world', apparatus theory loses sight of the error implied by the very notion of *mis*recognition (441). That is, Copjec insists, film theory overlooks Lacan's emphasis on the lure of visibility – the mistake made by the baby before the mirror. There is something other than the visible at stake in cinema, something which disturbs any identification between spectator and image on screen as well as the metaphorisation of the screen as a mirror. It is a disturbance which Copjec attempts to clarify via Nietzsche's insidious question: 'To everything which man allows to become visible, one is thus able to demand: what does he wish to hide?' (445).

From this point of view, the visible always raises the spectre of the hidden, the secret – a secrecy that, on this Lacanian reading, becomes inseparable from (structural to) the experience of looking as such. This is not, however, a secret that can be revealed by more scrutiny, more surveillance. On the contrary, the effect on the subject-spectator is that of something invisible, something missing, from the field of vision. This is what Lacan describes as the 'gaze', the concept that Copjec wants to distinguish from the idea of subjective looking with which it is so often equated. 'Behind the visual field,' she insists, following Lacan's *Seminar XI* in which he formulates his thinking on the gaze, 'there is, in fact, nothing at all' (450). The spectator may look, and look again – she is constituted as the desire to see/seek beyond the visible – but that 'nothing' ensures that her looking can never come to rest, can never find its object. Desire, so the argument goes, 'seeks after an impossibility', has no content. It is in from this point, then, that Copjec will recast the mirror – the imaginary, the cinema – as a screen against the void beyond the field of representation. Screen: defence, protection, façade on which the formations of fantasy are elaborated against nothing. (Compare Freud's first thoughts on fantasy as a form of protection – against memory, against helplessness – both in symptom and dream).

It is the idea of fantasy as a reaction-formation against that 'nothing' which drives what Stephen Heath has recently described as 'Žižek-film': an approach to the juncture between psychoanalysis and cinema associated with that of the Slovenian Lacanian School (Heath 1999: 36).[11] Certainly, some of the most vivid readings of cinema – from silent film to classic Hollywood to contemporary popular film – come through Žižek's work, its attention to the idea of fantasy in film as that which conceals something that cannot be symbolised, that veils an unbearable enigma. In effect, such an emphasis on veiling and screening displaces a tendency in film theory to equate looking with perception, identification with visibility (narcissistic recognition of one's like on screen: the dominant terms of feminist film theory, in fact). Describing Žižek's typical use of cinema to explicate Lacan's psychoanalysis, Heath recalls a telling instance of the difference of Žižek's pedagogy:

> Cinema can be called upon not just to furnish ways of translating; it itself *shows* and can be *shown to show*: "If a student asks 'What is the psychoanalytic Thing?' show him *Alien*," Žižek will exclaim in a lecture, arm flung screenward as the parasite viscously bursts through human flesh. This is an appeal to figuration of which Freud never dreamed ... cinema not as the vehicle of an exposition but as a matter of experience, on the edge of the real, at an extreme of psychoanalytic shock. (Heath 1999: 36)

We are back with shock – the spectacle of trauma – as the point of connection between psychoanalysis and cinema. But the terms are quite different, derived now from Lacan's elaboration of the concepts of the imaginary, the real, the symbolic. More precisely, *not* the imaginary. Like Copjec, Žižek is writing against what he perceives as the dominant trend in the English reception of Lacan, convinced that, in its focus on the imaginary, English Lacanianism 'has still not integrated all the consequences of the break marked by the seminar on *Ethics of Psychoanalysis* (1959-60)' (13). This must remain a question for scholars of Lacan. But in its insistence on a break between an 'early' (imaginary) and a 'late' (real/gaze) Lacan, the 'return to Lacan' in film theory interrupts the psychoanalysis of cinema in terms of the imaginary and/as institution that characterises both apparatus and (as we shall see) feminist film theory. *Interruption* because it is the specificity of cinema that seems to go missing in Žižek's account – the connivance between spectacle and image, projection and narrative, that is so much at issue for apparatus theory. 'What is proposed here,' he writes at the beginning of 'The Undergrowth of Enjoyment',

> is not some kind of 'applied psychoanalysis', a psychoanalytic reading of the products of culture, but on the contrary the articulation of some of the fundamental concepts of Lacanian psychoanalytic theory … by the use of examples taken from popular culture, and first from the cinema. (Žižek 1989: 14)

The ambition, and complexity, of the project is apparent. Part of Žižek's contribution to the psychoanalytic study of film is his turn to cinema as a way to question, and clarify, Lacan: the title of his edited collection of essays, *Everything You Always Wanted to Know about Lacan (But Were Afraid to Ask Hitchcock)*, exemplifies both theme and method. But Lacan is the *object* of interpretation, *not* cinema which is cast in the role of example, illustration, one form amongst others. (You might say that this is why Žižek can take on such a diverse range of films: cinema/film is not encountered in its singularity.) At the same time, Lacan is all too often invoked as a solution to the dilemmas and enigmas of culture: once explained – through the example of cinema, say, or popular literature – the explanatory force of his fundamental concepts seems to be taken for granted.

Such a taking for granted can generate a certain impatience with, or dismissal of, 'Žižek-film'. '"Hitchcock" here becomes no more than an element in a Lacanian theoretical procedure,' complains Richard Maltby in an exemplary response to Žižek's focus on Hitchcock's cinema (Maltby 1995: 437). Equally problematic is that this extension of the Lacanian frame of reference in film theory (an extension which can only be welcome) so often arrives in the form of a corrective: crudely, film theory has got Lacan 'wrong'. It is a gesture that can make it difficult both to keep hold of the questions driving Baudry and Metz and, more importantly, to engage with those aspects of apparatus theory which remain unexplored, unthought. Such an engagement must involve an extension of the frame of reference away from a near-exclusive focus on Freud and Lacan which has characterised psychoanalytic film theory. In this context, the imaginary may well have a key role to play. It is, for example, a conceptual bridge between the 'Lacanian' aspects of Metz's psychoanalysis of cinema and his approach to film as a 'good object' – an approach which brings Lacan into contact with both Melanie Klein and the object-relations tradition in psychoanalysis which has been so underused in psychoanalytic film theory.[12] At the same time, central to the current debates between psychoanalysis, feminism and Black Cultural studies, the imaginary brings to the fore the topic of cinema as a technique of aggression – a topic, and a technique, to which we will return in Chapter 5.

3 A BRIEF INTERLUDE: SCREENING FREUD

Under the influence of the technical procedure which I used at that time, the majority of my patients reproduced from their childhood scenes in which they were sexually seduced by some grown-up person. With female patients the part of seducer was almost always assigned to their father. (Freud 'An Autobiographical Study' (1925))

Cäcilie: You want us to be cured together?
Freud: Yes. And by one another.
(Jean-Paul Sartre, *The Freud Scenario* (1958))

Freud: I invented a theory to dishonour my father.
(*Freud – The Secret Passion* (John Huston, 1962))

One of the most powerful reflections on the origins of psychoanalysis comes through cinema: the remarkable encounter which took place between Jean-Paul Sartre and the American film director John Huston towards the end of the 1950s. 'Freud's descent into the unconscious should be as terrifying as Dante's descent into Hell,' Huston insists, commenting on his critically acclaimed *Freud – The Secret Passion*. 'With this in mind, Wolfgang [Reinhardt: Huston's producer] and I went to Paris to see Jean-Paul Sartre' (Huston, cited in Wollen 1999: 156). In keeping with what Jean-Bertrand Pontalis has identified as a typically

Hollywood tradition, Huston took Freud's '"heroic" period of discovery' as his starting-point – 'that key moment,' as Pontalis puts it in a brief commentary on Huston's film, 'when Freud abandoned hypnosis and gradually, painfully, invented psychoanalysis' (Sartre 1985: vii). 'I wanted to concentrate on that episode,' Huston recalled in interview in 1965, 'like a detective story' (*ibid.*: vii).

It is well known that Huston and Sartre fell out over this project. Huston wanted an 'intellectual suspense story', a scenario in which Freud was cast as adventurer (Fisher 1999: 129; Pontalis 1985: vii). Sartre's initial synopsis was accepted by Huston in December 1958. On receiving the screenplay, however, Huston asked for alterations and cuts; Sartre produced a still longer version for a film that would have run for about seven hours (the time of Hollywood is not that of psychoanalysis). A bitter dispute between the two men was followed by Sartre's removal from the project. 'Huston did not understand what the unconscious was' Sartre insisted, some years later, in an interview for *New Left Review* (Fisher 1999: 129). For his part, Huston referred to the risks in deciding to 'use someone like Sartre ... he really has no idea of what the film medium actually requires' (131). The final screenplay, as David James Fisher points out, 'was a hybrid creation' – a collaboration between Huston, Charles Kaufman and Wolfgang Reinhardt which took Sartre's version as its 'backbone' (Huston's term). On its release in 1962, *Freud* was a commercial failure.

Edited by Jean-Bertrand Pontalis, *The Freud Scenario* was first published four years after Sartre's death in 1984. Cutting across the history of psychoanalysis, of cinema, as well as Sartre's tangled relation to Freud, it is a monumental document. Pontalis' edition includes Sartre's first version of the screenplay (of 1959), together with a number of extracts from his first rewrite (1959-60), the original synopsis and a comparative table of the two versions. Sartre, at once engaged and repulsed by psychoanalysis, had immersed himself in the new documents which were becoming available from the Freud archives during the 1950s: the first volume of Ernest Jones' biography, for example, and the first, tendentiously edited, selection of Freud's letters to Wilhelm Fliess, *The*

Origins of Psychoanalysis.[1] 'There can be no doubt,' writes Pontalis, 'that these readings radically transformed Sartre's image of Freud'. Beginning in Charcot's Clinic at the Salpêtrière, *The Freud Scenario* is charged by Freud's struggle to find a way to understand his new ideas on memory and sexuality, fantasy and dream, as well as his experiments with therapeutic technique. In this sense, what Sartre attempts is a writing for cinema that is also a conceptual history of psychoanalysis. 'Pending the arrival of the image' (to borrow Pontalis's memorable phrase), *The Freud Scenario* offers a compelling vision of Freud, of cinema's resource when it comes to the experience of speech and cure, trauma and wish, at the origins of psychoanalysis.

The Freud Scenario may be the screenplay that cannot be screened, a story of Freud which cannot become cinema, but it is also a staging for cinema of Freud's attempt to understand the (sometimes obliterated) lives of the patients who found their way to his consulting-rooms through the 1880s and 1890s. The men and women who opened their minds to him were opening the everyday comfort of his rooms at Berggasse 19 onto scenes of primeval sex and violence – scenes which moved Freud to run the lives of his patients into the worlds of literature, folklore, and the occult. 'Imagine,' he writes to Fliess in January 1897, 'I obtained a scene about the circumcision of a girl. The cutting of a piece of the *labia minora* (which is still shorter today), sucking up the blood, following which the child was given a piece of the skin to eat' (Masson 1985: 227). This is an incredible scene, supposed to be a childhood memory, or a fantasy, told to Freud by one of his first hysterical patients, Emma Eckstein. What is she talking about? Freud is not sure. He orders the *Malleus Maleficarum* – the extraordinary 'Witches Hammer' of 1494 – and asks Fliess to recommend further reading on the Middle Ages (the devil and his 'cold' semen, dancing witches and their confessions, the vocabulary of popular songs). From another patient Freud learns that 'her supposedly otherwise noble and respectable father regularly took her to bed when she was from eight to twelve years old' (238). The story suggests to Freud that sexual shock can be a factor in the onset of mental illness, an element of the symptoms through which his patients are living. This is the beginning of his (still controversial) seduction theory. 'At the bottom of every case of hysteria,' Freud explained to the Society for Psychiatry and Neurology in Vienna in April 1896, 'there are one or more occurrences of premature sexual experience' (Masson 1984: 263).

Memory or fantasy? Trauma or wish? It is in terms of a decision between the two that the history of psychoanalysis is often told. More precisely, psychoanalysis emerges from Freud's hesitation between the two, his willingness to bear the indistinction between fiction and reality that the unconscious appears to bring in its wake. (Is this another kind of hallucination that is also a fact?) It is a hesitation that runs through Sartre's fiction – and, in particular, his exploration of Freud's treatment of the young hysteric, Cäcilie Körtner (a composite character supposed to be based, in part, on Anna O.).

Drawing on Freud's own relation to family and sexuality, medicine and self-analysis, Sartre's handling of this theme is marked by a conceptual and visual economy which makes itself felt throughout the three sequences we will discuss, briefly, here. The first (from Part III, Scenes 14-15) begins in Cäcilie's room where she is confined to her bed. She suffers the classic symptoms of hysteria. In particular, she is haunted by an image of herself as a prostitute – an image that she first gives to Freud in the form of a dream:

> *As she describes her dream, we see it as she describes it. We see a street at night: a gas-lamp illuminates it dimly. In the distance a woman who is Cäcilie, but whom we can barely make out, paces to and fro on the pavement. From a distance, she seems to be dressed like a classic prostitute.*
>
> Freud, *voice off*: Have you ever actually seen women walking the streets?
>
> Cäcilie, *voice off*: Of course.
>
> Freud, *voice off*: Were you dressed like them?
>
> Cäcilie, *voice off*: No.
>
> *Abruptly we see Cäcilie emerge from the shadows; she is wearing a wedding-dress, pure white, white veil, orange blossom. But her face*

is horribly painted, aged by a hard, exaggerated make-up, almost hideous.

        I had a wedding-dress on.

The wedding-dress, moreover, has an enormous tear in front, and through the rent her leg can be seen to above the knee.

        It's funny. It had a tear. That made me ashamed.

She paces to and fro on the pavement, in front of the street-lamp.

Freud, *voice off*:   Think a bit, Cäcilie. When did you see a torn wed-
                   ding-dress?

Cäcilie stops under the street-lamp and seems to be thinking.

Cäcilie, *voice off*: Never.

Freud, *voice off*:   Or other dresses?

Cäcilie, *voice off*: No! Yes. My mother's black dress. It got torn
                   yesterday, and Mama sat beside mending it while
                   I was reading.

The prostitute Cäcilie, as if satisfied by this reply, starts pacing up and down again. She passes in front of a carriage-entrance. In a dark corner, we suddenly perceive an alarming shadow: a motion-less man waiting.

'*As she describes her dream, we see it as she describes it*': Sartre's first direction for the scene in which Freud begins his treatment of Cäcilie puts the perceptual machinery of cinema at the disposal of psychoanalysis: the image on screen becomes an image of the dream. In other words, cinema becomes a type of dream screen, its special capacity for illusion miming the experience of the dream. In *The Freud Scenario*, we see the potential of that analogy between film and dream when it comes to cinema's repre-sentation of the analytic situation as such; in particular, Freud's classic request to Cäcilie: 'Well then, tell me what you dreamed' (*ibid.*: 298). On the one hand, at the level of the image, Sartre's scenario puts its spec-tators in the place of the dreaming Cäcilie: we *see* what she *dreams* as the hallucinatory world screens out Cäcilie's room. On the other hand, as voices off, Freud and Cäcilie evoke the analytic situation: an image of Cäcilie, 'lying with her head propped up on two pillows', Freud drawn near to her in a chair, is embedded in the dialogue which takes between them (294-8). Freud continues to question his patient. Suddenly we see Cäcilie – her dream-self – come to a halt; she stops walking as if in response to Freud's encouraging 'Think a bit, Cäcilie.' In other words, the dream-self pulls the dialogue of psychoanalysis into the dream, at the same time as she starts to join in the work of the analytic situation (question, answer, interpretation): 'The prostitute Cäcilie, as if satisfied by this reply, starts pacing up and down again'.

It is an uncanny moment. What we (would) see on screen is made to work with a voice-over in which the presence of *two* voices insists that the interpretation of the image, its 'truth', emerges through the insight and conflict of a dialogue. Struggling to understand what supports Cäcilie's image of herself as street-walker, Freud focuses on that 'alarming shadow' – the threat posed by a man who, in this (dream) version of events, accepts her advances before taking flight: 'He ran away and knocked me over' (300). That moment acts as a type of switch-point, flinging Cäcilie back into her childhood – represented, once again, by a screen-image compounded of dream and memory:

> Cäcilie has in fact fallen on the perron of her old villa. The carriage-entrance has disappeared. What is left is three steps leading to an open French window.
> Cäcilie is still in the wedding-dress, kneeling on one of the steps.
> French window, windows, steps are brightly lit: it is broad daylight. We can glimpse the interior that we know.
> Cäcilie is crying like a very young child, screwing up her face and sobbing violently.

The vicissitudes of that image in which a man pushes over a young woman-child govern the progress of Cäcilie's treatment. 'I'd hurt myself badly, falling on the perron' is Cäcilie's cue to Freud to treat this dream-image as a disguised memory, a message from childhood. He begins with the name given to Cäcilie in her dream, Potiphar – Pharoah's wife who was in love with Joseph. Joseph is the first name of both Breuer and Cäcilie's father.

So, Freud ventures to unpack the story embedded in that name: 'He [your father] pushed you when you were little. And you fell over?'

In Sartre's rendering of Freud's early practice, this is yet another façade. On his next visit, Freud probes further: 'So? Your father bumped into you and you fell over?' is the question confirmed by the image on screen, but refuted by Cäcilie's voice-over (Sartre keeps the conflict going):

In front of the villa, a little girl is climbing the steps of the perron. A man (Herr Körtner) rushes out and knocks her over.
Cäcilie, *voice off*: Oh! no.
Freud, *voice off*:   You told me so yesterday.
Cäcilie, *voice off, a touch of cynicism*:
                      Then I must have been lying.
Herr Körtner and the little Cäcilie have disappeared. The three steps and the sitting-room visible through the French window are deserted.
                      Didn't anyone tell you I was a terrible liar? I was running, I fell down; that's all ... My father carried me to the couch.
The father carries his daughter in his arms. He climbs the steps and is about to enter the sitting-room when Freud's sharp voice stops him in his tracks, with one foot in the air.
Freud, *voice off*:   Is that all?
Cäcilie, *voice off*: That's all.
Freud, *voice off*:   You're a liar, Cäcilie
The image disappears. We rediscover Freud sitting on his chair and bending forward, looking severely at Cäcilie.
Cäcilie, mesmerised, begins to protest. But Freud does not give her time.
                      A liar: you admitted it yourself. When you were on the couch, what happened to you?

'What happened to you?' The force of the question (one that Freud was reluctant to give up) is enough to stop a father in his tracks (the quasi-comic: *'Freud's sharp voice ... one foot in the air'*).[2] In other words, this is psychoanalysis (and cinema) as therapeutic intervention: through cinema, through the memory it claims to re-present, Freud's voice is able to conduct the image: to undo, or re-do, the past (Cäcilie's memory, her history). This is part of the drama of the early analytic situation – a drama that, as Gabbard and Gabbard point out in their extensive discussion of psychiatry and cinema, lends itself to cinematic representation: the theatrics connoted by the cathartic cure, 'the sudden and dramatic recovery from mental illness' as a forgotten, or repressed, memory comes to light (Gabbard and Gabbard 1987: 37).[3] In the classic scenario of the seduction theory, the memory in question must be one of sexual abuse:

> *Cäcilie, lying on the couch, looks in fascination at the eyes (invisible to us) of Herr Körtner, of whom we can see only the shoulders and the powerful neck.*
>> Remember, Cäcilie! Remember your terror. That's what made the date impossible to forget.
>
> *All of a sudden Herr Körtner bends down brutally over Cäcilie's face, which he masks; we can now see nothing but his head and broad shoulders. But it is obvious that he is kissing her on the lips.*
>
> *The vision, in any case, lasts only for a split second. At once Cäcilie's voice off rings out.*
>
> *(Great scream off from Cäcilie, terror – and in the terror itself a certain consent.)*
>
> *The vision disappears: we find ourselves back in the bedroom. Cäcilie is lying back on her pillows, terrified; Freud is bending over her.*
>
> *(In a certain way, these positions reproduce those of Herr Körtner and Cäcilie in the story just recounted.)*

This is the exchange that comes in answer to Freud's question: 'a father seduces a daughter' as Laplanche and Pontalis formalise the structure of the seduction theory (Laplanche and Pontalis 1986: 22). It is a scene, a 'vision' (a careful word: Sartre does not say memory), which appears to resist the cinematic image. On Sartre's direction, what Cäcilie sees is on screen for only a split second, the audience 'can now see nothing' as Herr Körtner approaches his daughter. It is the voice, a 'scream off', which comes to bear witness to an encounter that cannot be shown; only a scream can sustain the questionable mix of terror and consent that Sartre wants to find not only in this encounter between father and daughter but also in the relation between Cäcilie and Freud. At the level of the image, of gesture, this sequence insists on a coincidence between Freud and Herr Körtner, Cäcilie and the vision of Cäcilie masked by the body of her father, blanked from any but the screen of the mind.

On Sartre's telling, the abuse of a child-woman is transferred from father to Freud, from sexuality to interpretation. This important scene makes use of image and gesture to visualise the knot of symptom and technique, interpretation and desire, which Freud would have to confront throughout the 1890s. Freud may not be using hypnosis, but Sartre's Cäcilie is 'mesmerized', unable to resist the rhythm of the exchange between herself and Freud. She has no *time* to protest. Question, answer, question: Freud holds sway over both accusation and defence, while Cäcilie (in the place of a spectator) begins to see things which are not there. A vision, perhaps a memory – one with all the reality of perception – is conjured by the force of a question; in this, Sartre is capturing the *feel* of Freud's early practice, glimpsed between the lines of *Studies on Hysteria* as well as his letters to Fliess.[4] What does Freud want? What does he want (to hear) from Cäcilie, from his patients? Raising the spectre of psychoanalysis as a therapy that reproduces the terrors of Cäcilie's childhood, Sartre brings right to the fore the question of Freud's desire in the analytic situation.

A version of this sequence makes its way into Huston's *Freud* where, as Janet Walker points out in her reading of Sartre and Huston, incest is marked by a blank screen. 'A brief image of Herr Koertner followed by a child crying,' she notes, 'evokes the incestuous act at the same time that the blank screen insists on its cinematic unrepresentability' (Walker 1999: 173-4). In 1962, this is what cinema can show of Freud's insights into the sexual violence of family life. Flashback and voice-over – tools of memory and narrative in film – are used to construct the story of incestuous abuse. And, crucially, to reconstruct it. Following his self-analysis, Huston's Freud returns to Cecily's case, taking her back once again to the incident of assault. It is a scene in which Huston makes classic use of voice-over to establish Freud's narrative authority, to secure the image which, in this instance, runs below the voice: 'Shall I tell you a story?' Freud's question introduces the flashback which re-runs Cecily's molestation as a loving encounter with an 'accomplished and solicitous father' (174). This is, as Walker points out, Freud as *metteur en scène*, 'narrator of events at which he was not present' (74). The (only) voice that matters.

Sartre's Freud is not quite that. But it is only when Freud begins to tell, and question, his own dreams – only when the analytic encounter becomes a mutual enterprise between analyst and analysand – that psychoanalysis takes its distance from the image of assault. 'Well then, tell me what you dreamed': thus Sartre's Freud begins his work with Cäcilie. By the end, he is telling her his own in a sequence which brings Freud's self-analysis, his discovery of Oedipus, into the drama of Cäcilie's treatment:

> Freud: Oedipus is everybody. *(A pause.)*
> I must talk to you a bit about myself. In neuroses, I've viewed the parents as guilty and the children as innocent. That was because I hated my father. It's necessary to reverse the terms.
>
> Cäcilie: It's the children who are guilty!
>
> Freud, *smiling*: Nobody's guilty. But it's the children who ...
>
> *At these words, the hotel room. His mother opens the door softly, she glides noiselessly across to the bed.*
>
> I loved my mother, in every way: she fed me, she cuddled me, she took me into her bed and I was warm.
>
> *She slips between the sheets next to the child, after divesting herself of her dressing-gown; with his eyes closed and as if in his sleep, he cuddles up against her and clutches her round the neck with a jealous movement..*

I loved her in the flesh. Sexually.
The image disappears.
We find ourselves back in Cäcilie's room.
Cäcilie: You mean I was in love with my father?
He speaks as if to himself. He seems to be almost asleep.
Freud: I was jealous of mine because he possessed my
                 mother. I loved him and hated him at the same
                 time.
Cäcilie listens to him, but translates as she does so: it is her own
story she hears.

'It's the children who ...': the ellipsis in Freud's speech cues the image, the flashback that Maureen Turim has described as the 'juncture ... between present and past' in cinema (Turim, cited in Walker 1999: 177). At that juncture, Oedipus arrives on Freud's couch; the perverse father is displaced by the figure of a child in the grip of a fantasy that, as Freud had put it to Fliess in 1897, 'invariably seizes upon the theme of the parents' (Masson 1985: 264). 'They've not done with laughing at you, in Vienna!' is how Sartre's Fliess responds to Freud's new (equally unwelcome) theory. 'One day, it's the father who ravishes his daughter; the next, it's the daughter who wants to ravish her father' (Sartre 1985: 375).

It is an easy (though prevalent) caricature of Freud's struggle to understand the connection between what psychoanalyst Christopher Bollas has recently described as 'the imagined and the happened' in psychoanalysis (Bollas 1995: 103). By contrast, Sartre's Freud imports a more complex life and discipline (more precisely, the entanglement between life and discipline) into psychoanalytic studies in film. The publication of *The Freud Scenario* in 1985 has encouraged both psychoanalysis and film theory to engage with the passage from Sartre's screenplay(s) to Huston's *Freud*. It is a rare opportunity to view (some of) the process of writing and rewriting, vision and revision, between the different versions of *The Freud Scenario* and the version finally 'authorised' by cinema (Huston's film). No less than three essays in one of the most recent volumes on psychoanalysis and cinema – *Endless Night: Cinema and Psychoanalysis, Parallel*

Histories, edited by Janet Bergstrom, published in 1999 – take Freud/ Sartre/Huston as their point of focus. In particular, using the concept of 'textual trauma', Janet Walker sketches a model of reading which cuts across psychoanalytic, historical and feminist approaches to film. 'Specifically,' she writes, 'I am concerned with the difficulty that incest poses to the operations of scenarisation and censorship active both in Hollywood representation and in psychoanalytic approaches to sexuality' (Walker 1999: 172).[5] Attentive to the deletion, excision, and condensation which takes place between Sartre's screenplay(s) and Huston's film, Walker describes that work as a form of 'textual scarring' – a scarring which, by leaving its mark, gives 'covert expression to a deeply troubling subject'.

Is this a type of textual unconscious? An unconscious that the reader can trace back through the different versions of screenplay and film? Certainly, the juncture between *The Freud Scenario* and *Freud* opens up a space for film theory to begin to read across both psychoanalysis and cinema: *both* the representation of sexuality in psychoanalysis and the imaging of psychoanalysis and sexuality on screen. The vicissitudes of Freud's seduction theory represent a critical moment for psychoanalysis as theory, as therapy and as international institution. Following Sartre and Huston, it is a moment to which Hollywood also stakes its claim, its part in the cultural representation of psychoanalysis.

4   TYPICAL DREAMS

I have found, in my own case too, [the phenomenon of] being in love with my mother and jealous of my father, and I now consider it a universal event in early childhood, even if not so early as in children who have been made hysterical. (Freud to Wilhelm Fliess, 15 October 1897)

If there is no longer a father, why tell stories? Doesn't every narrative lead back to Oedipus? (Roland Barthes, *The Pleasure of the Text* (2000))

And so let us return to the point at the beginning of the film where this Oedipal itinerary, coinciding with the hero's trajectory, crystallises. (Raymond Bellour, 'Symbolic Blockage' (1975))

Does every narrative lead back to Oedipus? What does it mean to say so? There may be a pleasurable hubris in Barthes' question, his willingness to court the scandal of imposing Oedipus on the world(s) of narrative. But this is a question with a history in both psychoanalysis and film theory as disciplines that, in their different ways, turn to Oedipus as a figure who can stand for the desires embedded in dream, in cinema. 'Why Oedipus?' wonders Christopher Bollas in the course of a discussion of what he describes as the 'theatrical metaphor' at the heart of Freud's understanding of psychic conflict (Bollas 1994: 218). That is, why does Freud invoke a tragedy that, in its dramatisation of the ties between family and civic life, puts fiction on the inside of the psychoanalytic process? Coming before psychoanalysis, that fiction has a life of its own: Sophocles' *Oedipus Rex* is part of a complex world of myth and drama from which Freud, notoriously, selects his themes.[1] Coming *after* psychoanalysis, Oedipus will never be the same again. Freud's invention of Oedipus as wishful-murderous child is another contribution to the myth; or, in retelling the tragedy for twentieth-century culture, psychoanalysis finds a drama that will lend itself to cinema and film theory alike.

Oedipus: a typical dream?

'As a general rule,' Freud writes towards the beginning of his discussion of 'Typical Dreams' in *The Interpretation of Dreams*, 'each person is at liberty to construct his dream-world according to his individual peculiarities and so to make it unintelligible to other people'. The language of liberty and freedom signals Freud's defiance, his defence of the dream as a world apart (symbol of the right to a mind of one's own). Yet Freud himself is going to uncover a limit to that freedom at the very heart of dreaming. 'It now appears,' he continues, warming to his subject, 'that in complete contrast to this, there are a certain number of dreams which almost everyone has dreamt alike and which we are accustomed to assume must have the same meaning for everyone' (Freud 1900: 241).

The *same meaning* and *for everyone*? The very idea of a typical dream, it seems, is going to confirm the suspicion that psychoanalysis imposes a master plot on its various subjects; Oedipus, who kills his father and marries his mother, is the name of that plot. 'How many times,' asks Judith Mayne, in a key discussion of cinema and spectatorship in 1993,

> does one need to be told that individual film *x*, or film genre *y*, articulates the law of the father, assigns the spectator a position of male oedipal desire, marshals castration anxiety in the form of voyeurism and fetishism, before psychoanalysis begins to sound less like the exploration of the unconscious, and more like a master plot? (Mayne 1993: 68-9)

A sense of impatience with psychoanalytic film theory makes itself felt through this passage, an impatience that has become pervasive in film studies. The concepts of desire and castration, voyeurism and fetishism, have tended to dominate a psychoanalytic film theory that, taking Freud and Lacan as its primary points of reference, imports their focus on the Oedipus complex into the psychoanalysis of cinema. As was suggested at the end of Chapter 2, it is part of the ongoing project of psychoanalytic film theory to expand that frame of reference. At the same time, Freud's massive reworking of the idea of self, its relation to cultural life, remains largely underused (more precisely, un-contextualised) in film theory. To put this another way: the concepts which have become canonic, even over-familiar, in film theory – the imaginary, castration, voyeurism, identification, fantasy – can be revitalised by putting them back into the psycho-analytic texts from which they have been borrowed. As we will see in the following chapter, a number of feminist critics have undertaken that project of re-reading, re-contextualising (often through the problem of sexual difference). Similarly, it is worth going back to Freud's initial reflec-tions on Oedipus as what, in *The Interpretation of Dreams*, he calls a 'typical dream' – a form of dreaming which is crucial to the movement of psychoanalysis outside of the consulting room. On the one hand, the scenario is familiar. As the parricidal, and incestuous, dream of European culture, *Oedipus Rex* will shift Freud's focus from the traumatised children of the seduction theory to the libidinal child of the Oedipus complex. On the other hand, the idea of the 'typical' opens psychoanalysis up to the question of culture – to what, as Lacan might put it, is 'in' the dreamer more than him or her (Lacan 1979: 263).

Such a question is on Freud's mind throughout his discussion of 'Typical Dreams' which begins with a careful, perhaps frustrated, acknowledge-ment of the limitations of psychoanalytic therapy. 'We are not in general,' Freud notes, 'in a position to interpret another person's dream unless he is prepared to communicate to us the unconscious thoughts that lie behind its content' (Freud 1900: 241). It is a severe restriction, but one that Freud is keen to counter with his 'special interest' in typical dreams: dreams which, arising 'from the same sources in every case', promise to extend the reach of psychoanalytic interpretation into collective and cultural life. However, the promise looks doomed to disappointment. When we try to interpret a typical dream, Freud explains, the dreamer's associations become 'obscure and insufficient' – as if he or she is possessed by a meaning which belongs somewhere else, which cannot be understood in terms of the dreamer's *own* interpretative work. In other words, the typical dream threatens to bring psychoanalysis to a halt at the very moment it appears to extend its 'practical applicability', to borrow Freud's phrase (*ibid.*). In fact, Freud finds himself obliged to change the fundamental rule of psychoanalysis. In the case of the typical dream, the interpretation of the analysand's free associations has to be supplemented with what Freud will describe later as a 'combined technique': a technique that 'on the one hand rests on the dreamer's associations and on the other hand fills the gaps from the interpreter's knowledge of symbols' (353). That is, the psychoanalyst has to supply an interpretation of the symbolic, or cultural, dimensions of the dream. No wonder that Freud maintains that the analyst 'can make nothing of a large amount of his material' if he does not feel at home in the study of the 'history of civilisation, mythology, the psychology of religion and the science of literature' (Freud 1926: 246).

In other words, the idea of the typical (the master plot) opens psychoanalysis onto the scene of an unconscious which does not belong to the wishful-shameful intimacies of individual life. There is, Freud discovers, the potential for a coincidence between dream and culture (or culture, like the dream, can be the royal road to the unconscious). On this reading, the master plot is not what is imposed by psychoanalysis but what psychoanalysis shares with the various cultures which sustain its vision, its forms of interpretation. What the psychoanalyst Jean Laplanche describes as 'extra-mural psychoanalysis' – psychoanalysis as a cultural movement, psychoanalysis as it comes into contact with 'cultural phenomena' – is also there in the consulting-room, the clinical realm that defines psychoanalysis as a therapy (Laplanche 1989: 11-12). To put this another way, a psychoanalysis of culture is possible because 'culture' is already a part of psychoanalysis. Or, an 'exploration of the unconscious' (Mayne) and the (re)discovery of a master plot may be one and the same thing.[2]

In this sense, Oedipus is the name that Freud gives to one of the most powerful, and prevalent, narratives on the cusp between culture and the unconscious. It is the name of a family romance introduced under the sign of the 'typical' in one of the most unsettling discussions in *The Inter-pretation of Dreams*. Towards the end of the nineteenth century, part of the force and controversy of Freud's thinking derives from his relentless probing of what he describes as the 'real relations' between parents and children (Freud 1900: 256). 'We must distinguish,' he insists, 'between what the cultural standards of filial piety demand of this relation and what everyday observation shows it in fact to be'. Freud's discussion of typical dreams bears witness to his assault on that piety, the variety of bloody family plots with which he was prepared to contend. Alongside Oedipus, Kronos (who devoured his children) and Zeus (who emasculated his father) make their appearance. A young married woman beating on her body with her fists to kill the unborn infant inside is another striking figure. Years later, her wish for the death of her child fuels a dream in which the woman (now a mother) sees her (now much loved) daughter lying dead 'in a case'. Nothing here, it seems, to give Freud pause: not wanting a child, killing a child, may be nearly the same thing in the (some-times ruthless) world of wishes.

It is in this context that Freud introduces his well-known, if largely unwelcome, analysis of Sophocles' *Oedipus Rex* as a privileged example of a new category of dreams: 'Dreams of the Death of Persons of Whom the Dreamer is Fond' (248). Not all such dreams, Freud clarifies, can be described as typical. Those dreams in which a loved one dies but the dreamer feels no grief conform to Freud's previous discussion of the dream as a fulfilment of a repressed wish to be uncovered through the dreamer's free associations ('the affect felt in the dream belongs to its latent and not to its manifest content' (248-9)). Only those dreams in which the dreamer feels the pain of loss that she would expect to experience in her waking life belong to the category of the typical. 'The meaning of such dreams,' Freud concludes, with apparent confidence, 'as their content indicates, is a wish that the person in question may die' (249). What Freud is dealing with, then, is a form of dreaming which sidesteps the distinction between manifest and latent content (the very distinction that, as we saw in Chapter 2, he has laboured so hard to establish). By contrast, typical dreams wear their hearts on their sleeve; a loved one dies, the dreamer wishes for the death of that loved one (a parent, a child, a sibling).

No surprise, perhaps, that Freud expects protests from his readers at this interpretation of their commonplace dreams. In response to that protest, he turns to the figure of Oedipus to help reconstruct a 'portion of the vanished mental life of children': the child in the dreamer, so to speak (250). One of the founding works in the (European) ideal of an international literature, *Oedipus Rex* is evidence, for Freud, that it is the 'fate of all of us, perhaps, to direct our first sexual impulse towards our mother and our first hatred and our first murderous wish against our father' (262). *Perhaps*, Freud writes. That is, his interpretation of Sophocles' drama is both confident and tentative; at this stage, Freud is trying to find a way to think about the loving murderousness which appears to dominate the psychic life of the child (assumed to be a boy). As Freud writes to Fliess on 15 October 1897, in one of his first references to Oedipus:

> We can understand the gripping power of *Oedipus Rex*, in spite of all the objections that reason raises against the presuppositions of fate ... the Greek legend seizes upon a compulsion which everyone recognises because he senses its existence within himself. Everyone in the audience was once a budding Oedipus in fantasy and each recoils in horror from the dream fulfilment here transplanted into reality with the full quantity of repression which separates his infantile state from his present one. (Masson 1985: 272)

This is one of Freud's clearest statements on the link between dream and drama: drama as the realisation of the dream-wish ('the dream fulfilment here transplanted into reality'). Theatre, it seems, is a type of real dream, from which the spectator may well recoil in horror even as he is compelled to recognise himself and his wishes. Part of the work of Sophocles' play is to bring those wishes to consciousness, to bring to the stage a character that can stand in for every member of the audience. 'There must be something,' Freud confirms, returning to the topic of *Oedipus Rex* in his discussion of typical dreams,

> which makes a voice within us ready to recognise the compelling force of destiny in the *Oedipus*. [...] His destiny moves us only because it might have been ours – because the oracle laid the same curse upon us before our birth as upon him. It is the fate of all of us, perhaps, to direct our first sexual impulse towards our mother and our first hatred and our first murderous wish against our father. Our dreams convince us that that is so. King Oedipus, who slew his father Laïus and married his mother Jocasta, merely shows us the fulfilment of our own childhood wishes. (Freud 1900: 262)

On Freud's reading, *Oedipus Rex* is staging the very drama that psycho-analysis is going to uncover in the domains of symptom and dream (a coincidence which accounts for the fact that this ancient drama continues to move a modern audience). Like the process of psychoanalysis, the action of *Oedipus Rex* is there to reveal the truth of its wishes to that audi-ence. The play, and the poet, speak to a 'voice within us'; we are moved because we know that it could have been us, up there on stage, cursed by an oracle that has guessed at the desire for love and murder of which, in our dreams, in our childhood, we are all guilty: 'Our dreams convince us that it is so'. In other words, it is the dream-self, the child-self, who is gripped by the power of dramatic representation; what we find in drama, as in the dream, are a wish and a child who refuses to give way on what he has once longed for.

Tracking his way back to that child, Freud marks the place of the spec-tator as one of compulsion: towards murder and incest ('the Greek legend seizes upon a compulsion which everyone recognises') as well as identi-fication and recognition (the poet 'compels us to recognise our own inner minds' (263). In Freud's initial responses to Sophocles' *Oedipus Rex*, then, we can glimpse an outline of the semiotics of reading that is going to support psychoanalytic film theory. Freud does not treat *Oedipus Rex* – or, indeed, Oedipus – as a 'record of symptoms' (a treatment which, as

E. Ann Kaplan points out, has been associated with some of his followers (Kaplan 1990: 2)). In fact, there is no complex to be diagnosed in the play; its wishful fantasy, as Freud puts it, is not repressed but realised. Nor does he confine himself to a thematic reading. What *Oedipus Rex* says and does is crucial, the material of Freud's analysis. But, from the very beginning, Freud wants to link the themes of Oedipus' tragedy (murder, incest) to the place of the spectator in the action of the play. Who, or what, is Oedipus speaking *to*? What is set in motion in the spectator by the action of the play? (What, as Baudry might put it, is its subject effect?)

It is a subject-effect that, on Freud's reading, pulls in 'everyone in the audience'. Oedipus is a figure who crosses the boundary between culture and dream, whose destiny will determine Freud's account of the origins of cultural life in the (boy) child's renunciation of incest (with the mother) and murder (of the father). Freud will not introduce the concept of the Oedipus complex into his published writings until 1910 (in an essay on 'A Special Type of Choice of Object Made by Men'). Nevertheless, his conviction that the child's libidinal life is worked through the experience of love and rivalry in the family guides his work from the end of the 1890s. As Freud returns to, and refines, his concept, the Oedipus myth is used to describe an *organisation* of relations within the family, as well as the relation between the sexes. Above all, on Freud's model it is what happens to the Oedipus complex that is going to determine the child's access to sexuality, to sexual difference and to cultural life. That is, the story of the Oedipus complex in psychoanalysis is the story of how a child takes on an identity as son or daughter, as boy or girl, as heterosexual or homosexual, conformist or rebel. Amidst the clamour of his oedipal loves and hates, the child has to find a place for himself – as a boy, let us say. He wishes to be like his father, Freud suggests; that is, the boy identifies with his father, takes him as an ideal. He loves his mother, puts her in the place of a loved object. But, in the conjugal family, the mother 'belongs' to the father. She becomes the first site of conflict between the father and a son who is faced with the paradox of the Oedipus complex: be like your father (be a man, love a woman) but also do not be like your father (you may not have all that your father has; you may not wish for your mother).

This is the classic double bind of what has become known as Oedipal law, imposed by the father on the son via the fear of castration – one of the most notorious ideas in the Freudian canon. 'In boys,' Freud maintains,

> the [Oedipus] complex is not simply repressed, it is literally smashed to pieces by the shock of threatened castration. Its libidinal cathexes are abandoned, desexualised and in part sublimated; its objects are incorporated into the ego, where they form the nucleus of the super-ego and give that new structure its characteristic quali-ties. In normal, or, it is better to say, in ideal cases, the Oedipus complex exists no longer, even in the unconscious; the super-ego has become its heir. Since the penis ... owes its extraordinarily high narcissistic cathexis to its organic significance for the propagation of the species, the catastrophe to the Oedipus complex (the aban-donment of incest and the institution of conscience and morality) may be regarded as a victory of the race over the individual. (Freud 1925a:257)

All this because the little boy loves his penis more than his mother? (And his father, his sister, his brother.) Loving the penis, loving the 'race', amounts to the same thing here; or, as various critics have pointed out, masculine narcissism is the very ground of Freud's theory of culture.[3] Heir to the Oedipus complex, the super-ego – internal representative of the father's law, vehicle of conscience and culture – depends on the fact that the boy has something to lose: crudely, because he fears the loss of his penis, the boy renounces both his rivalry with his father and his homosexual desire for him. Instead, he is shocked into identification with the father's threat, his prohibition – and so internalises the law that, for Freud, is the very foundation of culture.

The romance will become ever more involved as Freud develops his account of the 'complete' Oedipus complex, and begins to wonder how it might all be different for girls. As Laplanche and Pontalis point out in their invaluable *The Language of Psycho-Analysis*, Freud's gradual elab-oration of the Oedipus complex is 'in reality coextensive with that of psychoanalysis itself' (Laplanche and Pontalis 1973: 283). A huge task. But, as far as film theory is concerned, it is the idea of the Oedipus complex as a story of family and the origins of identity, of desire and the (paternal) law which comes to counter it, that has been decisive. 'Isn't storytelling always a search for origins,' muses Roland Barthes, in response to Murnau's classic *City Girl* (1929), 'an account of one's entanglements with the Law, an entry into the dialectic of tenderness and hate?' (Barthes, cited in Bellour 2000: 77). It is this notion of Oedipus – coextensive with narrative and identity – that film theory will engage through its exploration of the diversity as well as predictability of narrative cinema. 'The film,' writes Stephen Heath in 'Film Performance' in 1977, 'is developed and exploited from the photograph as an alternative and successor to the novel for the production-reproduction of the *novelistic*. [...] The title of the novelistic is *Family Romance*' (Heath 1981: 125). This is a vision of cinema as what Heath describes elsewhere as a type of family machine – 'family relations taken as the arena of the social-individual construction-placing and of the necessary containment ... of action' (239). A key triangle emerges here between novel, cinema and psychoanalysis: in their different ways, all three can be described as family romances, family industries. As Constance Penley has recently pointed out, an 'Oedipally fueled fantasy' of the heterosexual couple (the first step towards the conjugal family) remains a staple of American cinema. Cinema can form and deform that fantasy but it remains a type of matrix within which the various configurations of fantasy life are played out.[4]

For now, let us just note that the woman is bound to play a pivotal role in the Oedipal scenario: horror at the sight of this 'mutilated creature' helps to confirm the reality of the father's threat of castration (Freud 1925a: 252). In other words, an image of the woman (an image of castration) binds the boy to paternal law. It is a point to which feminist film theory will return, bringing into focus the concepts of voyeurism and disavowal, helping to secure Freud's account of the Oedipal narrative. For one powerful strand of psychoanalytic film theory, however, that narrative will become a key site to the interpretation of Oedipus, the family romance to which he lends his name, as the dream of classic Hollywood cinema.

Textual dreaming

'I merely believe in the law.'
(Mitch Brenner to Melanie Daniels, *The Birds* (Alfred Hitchcock 1969))

Writing in 1979, Raymond Bellour, the theorist whose name has been most closely associated with the unveiling of Oedipal fantasy in film, offered a brief sketch of the cultural and sexual formations supporting the Oedipus of both psychoanalysis and cinema:

> This configuration is founded on the relation of narcissistic doubling between man and woman. From the end of the eighteenth century and throughout the nineteenth, from which we are barely emerging, this doubling rules the two sexes' relations of desire. From it psychoanalysis is born – first Freudian, then Lacanian – using the univocal model of Oedipus and castration to organise conflict and sexual difference around the restricted scene of the nuclear family. Thus one finds this configuration in most Western films, especially in classical American cinema, which (as has often been remarked) seems to have given itself the object of leading back through the great novelistic heritage of the nineteenth century and everything in it that continues to compel us. (Bellour 2000: 12)

This dense, and wide-ranging, passage summarises Bellour's decisive intervention in the field. Psychoanalysis, cinema and the novel converge in their exploration, and representation, of family, sexuality and culture in the modern period, while the Oedipal model of desire and narrative which Bellour claims to uncover in cinema (as in psychoanalysis, as in the nineteenth-century novel: Bellour has written extensively on the Brontës) is 'historical through and through' (12). That is, Oedipus is bound to the forms of sexuality and sexual difference, to the structures of family and society, which emerge in the modern period – and, Bellour insists, continue to be played out on the screens of our cinema.[5] In her preface to the recent edition of his essays on cinema, *The Analysis of Film*, Constance

Penley underlines the consistency, and innovation, of Bellour's contribution to film studies. She begins her brief commentary on that contribution by simply listing the range of nineteenth- and twentieth-century texts on which Bellour has worked: film, photography, video, novels, interviews, diaries, critical editions. What links these diverse topics, Penley suggests, is Bellour's own fascination with his themes – a 'fascinated familiarity with films', as Bellour describes it, which he situates as part of the very process of cultural analysis (2).

The ideas of fascination, desire, and obsession recur in Bellour's attempts to characterise what it is about film that drives him to the methodical, and painstaking, work of analysis. In this sense, Bellour is a critic who responds to Metz's challenge to the theorist to investigate his own imaginary, to situate his desire in relation to the object – film, cinema – he aims to know (Metz 1982). The question of desire in the critic, the spectator, the film is a starting-point, then, for this psychoanalysis of cinema. And, in particular, for the classic psychoanalyses of Hitchcock's cinema which established Bellour as a key figure in psychoanalytic film theory. In particular, essays devoted to *The Birds* ('System of a Fragment' 1969), *North by Northwest* ('Symbolic Blockage' 1975), *Marnie* ('To Enunciate' 1977), *Psycho* ('Psychosis, Neurosis, Perversion' 1979) helped to set the terms of the debate for a psychoanalysis of film preoccupied by the tangled relations among narrative and image, subjectivity and sexuality. In the first instance, Bellour laid the foundations for a textual analysis of film: 'shot by shot, sequence by sequence', as Penley points out. Exhaustive, obsessive (Bellour's word), such an analysis is marked by a prevalence of the image – both frame and sequence – on the page: Bellour's shot-by-shot analysis of Melanie Daniels's arrival at Bodega Bay in *The Birds*, for example, or the 66 frames from *Psycho* which organise the discussion of 'Psychosis, Neurosis, Perversion'. The idea of 'text' here is also specific, part of Bellour's dialogue with what he describes as Roland Barthes' 'utopic expansion' of text in his studies of narrative through the 1960s and 1970s. 'From Work to Text', first published in 1971, as well as *S/Z* (1970), Barthes' book-length study on Honoré de Balzac's story of the castrato, *Sarrasine*, are two powerful influences on Bellour's approach to film. The model for Barthes' idea of reading as an activity, a process of production rather than consumption, is *play*. The reader of a text – the term which skews a more traditional understanding of 'work', the authored volume on the shelf, supposed to yield meaning(s) – is caught up in a network of words and codes, references and echoes, which may be known, or half-known, but which can never be brought to rest (along the lines of 'this means that'). On the contrary, Barthes compares his reader to 'someone at a loose end (someone slackened off from any imaginary)', a subject out for a 'stroll' in the world of words. 'What he perceives,' Barthes concludes, 'is multiple, irreducible, coming from a disconnected, heterogeneous variety of substances and perspectives' (Barthes 1977: 159).

This image of the reader as a type of *flâneur* can seem at odds with the work undertaken by Bellour – 'to the point of obsession, a methodical kind of work,' as he acknowledges in 'A Bit of History' (Bellour 2000: 15). But it may be that that method – tenacious, painstaking: Bellour is at the editing table, viewing the film shot by shot, stopping and starting the movement of the image – is the other side of the fascination, or play, that sparks the analysis of a film. This is, Penley suggests, a 'new form of creative play with the image', and it pushes film analysts towards new ways of writing about what they are doing with film. Bellour himself writes of an occasion, in spring 1967, on which he and Christian Metz decided to collaborate on an analysis of Hitchcock's *Suspicion*. Having settled on the 'train scene', in which the diegetic couple (Cary Grant and Joan Fontaine) meet for the first time, the analytic couple (Metz and Bellour) watched the sequence several times. In vain. 'Nothing,' Bellour recalls. 'No desire for analysis. No desire for anything. There was a sort of denseness before the object'. It is a revealing story. No desire, no play – means no work, no *analysis*. It is as if the very rigour of Bellour's textual analysis, the demand made on the film analyst to *produce* the text on which he is working, can only be sustained by a fascination strong enough to meet that demand. At the very least, there must be a wish to look at and *know* the film: to view, describe and analyse the articulation of camera shots in a particular film or fragment of film; to reconstruct the pattern, if any, which emerges from that articulation, as well as the articulation between sequences; to reconstruct the narrative pattern, or system, of the film from such a breakdown of its elements.

Consider, as one example, the different levels of Bellour's analysis of a short sequence from Hitchcock's *The Birds*. It is the scene in which Melanie Daniels arrives at Bodega Bay to deliver a pair of lovebirds (a surprise birthday present) to Mitch Brenner's house. The sequence, Bellour notes, lasts six minutes and 15 seconds. The time of analysis, however, is of a very different order. First, Bellour divides the sequence into two series, A and B, which begin with Melanie's departure from the pier in Bodega Bay, track her journey to the Brenner house and then her return, with Mitch, back to the bay. To aid the reader in following his shot by shot breakdown (an apposite word) of the sequence, Bellour offers the following summary:

SHOT	
3-12	Departure
12-14 (A0)	Melanie on the boat
15-24 A1	The boat, paddled by Melanie, approaching the dock
25-31 A2	Melanie's progress to the house on the dock
32-36 A3 (Center A)	Melanie in the house
37-43 A4	Melanie toward the boat on the left
44-56 A5-B1	Melanie in the boat
56-60 B2 (Center B)	Melanie in the boat; Mitch looking at Melanie
60-71 B3	Melanie in the boat, Mitch in the car
72-84	Arrival

To read this is, I think, to begin to grasp what Bellour means when he suggests that 'analysis of itself generates a second text' on which the analyst of film then sets to work (137). It is an effort which involves a type of 'double transgression', Bellour acknowledges, 'in which the film is constituted as text and, from there, a text is constituted' (17). Resisting reduction to the world of words on the page, any attempt to recapture the 'flesh and bones' of cinema, the experience of viewing, risks turning film into novel – a 'first restriction in principle on the power of analysis', as Bellour puts it (30). Running against that restriction, he offers a remarkable new text: a description of the succession and combination of shots, of camera position and object of vision, of dialogue, reproduced alongside the 84 stills which constitute the Bodega Bay sequence in 'System of a Fragment'. Take, for example, the well-known sequence (shots 73-82) in which Melanie is attacked by a gull:

73	MOVING FULL SHOT Camera moves in on pier as off-screen Melanie approaches it.	Pier	Movement	Distant
74	CLOSE-UP Melanie smiling.	Melanie seeing	Static (close-up)	Close
75	MOVING LONG SHOT Camera moves in on pier as Mitch appears from background and camera pans right with his run to edge of pier, where he stands waiting.	Mitch seen	Movement	Distant
76	CLOSE-UP Melanie smiles, then her slightly tilted face sets.	Melanie seeing	Static	Close
77	FULL SHOT Sky with seagull in flight from foreground left off-screen background right.	Seagull	Static	Distant Close
78	CLOSE SHOT On Melanie, gull flies from right foreground, strikes her head, and leaves to background right.	Melanie, gull	Static	Close
79	FULL SHOT Gull flies from right foreground to toward left background.	Seagull	Static	Distant

80	LONG SHOT Mitch, strolling on the pier, stares closely at Melanie, off-screen.	Mitch seeing	Static	Distant
81	CLOSE SHOT Melanie, who had raised her hand to her head, removes it and looks at glove.	Melanie seen-seeing	Static	Close
82	CLOSE-UP (INSERT) Blood on index finger of Melanie's gloved hand.	Melanie (her finger)	Static close-up	Close

What is this text? As Judith Mayne points out, one of the most vociferous complaints against textual analysis is its creation of a 'film text that has only the most remote connection with the ways in which films are actually received' (Mayne 1993: 105).

As we have seen, Bellour is only too aware of this. In fact, that viewing and analysis are remote from one another may be inevitable given that what the analyst is trying to understand is *how* the film engages the spectator – pulls him into the activity of viewing, over and over again. Bellour begins at the beginning, with the 'tiny fragments', the single elements, of film which can be listed, numbered, described (Bellour 2000: 29). In this sense, part of the challenge of Bellour's method is its radical singularity. It can be difficult to follow the twists and turns of a reading so close to and yet so distant from its object – a reading which, as Bellour writes in the introduction to 'System of a Fragment', takes off from the 'logical accident of a fascination' (29). A fascination with the secrets of the system, a sequence, a shot. This is the material of his analysis, the constitutive elements that enable him to see something.

At its most simple, Bellour suggests, we can see the system of classical cinema in an alternation, an opposition, between two shots: 'Melanie seeing/what Melanie sees', in the case of the Bodega Bay sequence (shots 74-75 are one example of this) (50). In other words, the film *narrates* through alternation, through the movement between observer and the object of his or her vision.

Tracking that alternate movement with infinite care, Bellour will extend, and disperse, its reach. 'We must see it where it is at work,' he insists in 'To Alternate/To Narrate' in 1980, 'orchestrated, orchestrating all levels – in the classical cinema' (262). More specifically, that 'web of plots stamped with the name Alfred Hitchcock' (29). It is an ambitious project, one that takes Bellour through the detailed 'rhyme' of shots which orchestrate Hitchcock's filming, through which his cinema will materialise. Take, for example, Bellour's commentary on the four static shots 76-79:

> They alternate two shots of Melanie (76 and 78) with two of gulls (77 and 79). But a double variation complicates this simple alternation of static shots. The first relates to a change in the object of vision: Mitch, who has just appeared on the pier (75), then the gull that crosses the sky (77). Shot 76 juxtaposes them: the disappearance of the smile that has been on Melanie's face since shot 72 marks the change. The second variation relates to the conjunction seeing/seen (or seeing/seeing) in the same framing: in shot 77 the gull strikes Melanie on the head. This confirms a correspondence between Mitch and the gull or, to be exact, between Mitch's look and the gull. [...] As the centres slide beneath one another, the two successions of shots are superimposed: as Mitch hurries onto the pier, the gull descends on Melanie; the bird of the gift appears in its baleful double. (59)

Thus Bellour begins to address the problem of how, as he puts at the beginning of his reading of *The Birds*, 'meaning emerges in the succession of a story in pictures' (28). Alternation, repetition, variation: it is in these terms that Bellour describes the progress of the sequence through the rhythm of continuity (shot/reverse-shot) and its interruption, of stasis and movement, of close and distant. Above all, it is the idea of rhyme, or pattern, which supports Bellour's exploration of the formal and conceptual homologies layered through Hitchcock's cinema: at the level of the shot, the relations of symmetry and substitution (the gull for Mitch in shots 75 and 77, for example); the correspondence between shots across the whole field of the film text (the close-up on Melanie's gloved hand in shot 82 in this sequence harks back to shot 33, its close focus on Melanie's hands as she leaves a letter for Cathy in the Brenner household); at the level of the plot, the shift from the loving birds which mark the initial encounter between Melanie and Mitch to the aggression unleashed by the birds (or *The Birds*) in Bodega Bay.

It is through his analysis of the construction and combination of shots that Bellour explores the puzzle of that shift, tracking the symbolic violence of the close-up in shot 82 back through the sequence he has identified as central to the film. It is not possible to reproduce that reading here, but the correspondence established between Mitch and the gull in shots 75 and 77, 79 and 80, suggests the line of enquiry: 'The fact,' as Bellour concludes, 'that it is impossible for Mitch and Melanie to see each other as seen without opening up a dual and murderous relationship' (63). Such attention to the sexuality and aggression of the look indicates the value of Bellour's analysis for feminist film theory. But it is the problem of how to establish the heterosexual couple – 'the route that leads Melanie to Mitch', in Bellour's terms – which will guide his exploration of looking and desire through the film. Hitchcock leaves his audience in no doubt that a (for some, perhaps, platitudinous) reference to Oedipus governs his plot: on the face of it, the obstacle which confronts Melanie and Mitch is his mother, Lydia – 'afraid of any woman who can give Mitch what she can't', as Annie, a previous rival for his love, explains to Melanie on her arrival in Bodega Bay.[6] Annie's account is given ('with all due respect to Oedipus') as a warning. The relation between Lydia and Mitch represents a type of 'symbolic blockage' to borrow the phrase that Bellour will use to describe another of Hitchcock's mother-son couples: the relation between Clara Thornhill and her son, Roger, in *North by Northwest* ('Thornhill is nothing but a big baby, and only Cary Grant could confer on him the equivocal status of a man of 40 and an ill-grown adolescent' (84)). In other words, Brenner (like Thornhill) takes up his place in what Bellour describes as the Hitchcockian fable: the hero is caught up in a 'play' of terror and desire (an ordeal, an enigma: the attack by the birds, the mistaken identity of *North by Northwest*) which, by forcing him to symbolise the

relationship that links him to his mother, will carry him towards possession of a wife (the mode of substitution – of one woman for another, in this
case – which helps to identify Bellour's concept of the symbolic).

In his monumental reading of *North by Northwest*, Bellour is able
to trace that itinerary – one that, he insists, 'may justifiably be called
"Oedipal"' – from the opening scenes of the film (Thornhill is seized by
Vandamm's men as he gets up to send a message to his mother) to its well-
known conclusion: the final shots of the train entering a tunnel following
the love scene between Eve and Thornhill. Bellour recalls Hitchcock's
comment on that shot in 1959: 'It's a phallic symbol. But you mustn't tell
anyone' (81). As horror film, however, *The Birds* presents a different 'resolution' to its complex. The problem posed by sexuality and sexual difference through the narrative, the difficulty of bringing Mitch and Melanie
together, is mapped onto the film's distinction between 'good and bad
birds' – as Bellour argues in his (remarkably schematic) discussion of the
conclusion of the film in 'System of a Fragment' (66). But the concluding
sequence of *The Birds* is, as Jacqueline Rose points out in her response
to Bellour's Oedipal reading of Hitchcock's film, 'abortive'. Melanie is
reduced to a state of catatonia: speechless, shocked, she is in the mother's arms at the close of the film (Rose 1976-77: 97-8). In other words,
horror reworks – reforms, deforms – the family romance to include what
Bellour describes as the 'phantasm' of the birds.

To put all this another way: when, in 1975, Bellour identified the guiding
principle of Hitchcock's *oeuvre* as one in which an ordeal 'leads the hero –
or heroes – from the enigma to its resolution, from error to recognition', he
was opening up a space for Oedipus in psychoanalytic film theory (77). It
is not only that Hitchcock's cinema is wedded to the connection between
sexuality and death (*Psycho* is only the most obvious example), and popu-
lated by Oedipal sons (again, of course, Norman Bates, but Mitch and
Thornhill are two compelling instances). But in his emphasis on the hero's
itinerary from enigma to resolution, Bellour also brings into focus an
aspect of Oedipus of which Freud makes relatively little in *The Interpretation of Dreams*. Having unknowingly slain his father, King Laïus, in a
sudden quarrel, Oedipus travels onto Thebes where, as Freud notes,

he 'solved the riddle set him by the Sphinx who barred his way' (Freud 1900, *SE IV*: 261). In return, he is offered Jocasta's (his mother's) hand in marriage. That is, following his solution of the riddle of the Sphinx – 'this monster, a woman with the body of a beast' as Michèle Montrelay puts it – Oedipus, already a parricide, is plunged into incest (Montrelay 1978: 260). It is as a solver of riddles, then – more strongly, of the puzzle of the monstrous feminine – that Oedipus marries his mother, becoming both father and brother to their children. And it is as a solver of riddles – the enigma of cinema – that Oedipus symbolises the place of the analyst-spectator in Bellour's theory. 'Through its *mise-en-abîme*,' Bellour concludes his study of *North by Northwest*, 'the generalised rhyme of the classical film presumes, in its final textual effect, the fascinated desire of the analyst' (Bellour 2000: 192). Fascination, again. The fascination of textual analysis that, in the desirous activity of its production, its desire to explore and know a system embroiled in our 'typical dreams', comes in response to one dominant form of cinema: Hollywood, the 'classical' cinema of the family romance.

•

5   THE WOMAN IN QUESTION

Finally, and more simply, I ask the question, why is the woman attacked? (Jacqueline Rose, 'Paranoia and the Film System' (1976))

The question of pleasure has been a crucially troubling one for feminist film theory and filmmaking, and the theory of the apparatus appears to answer the question before it is even raised. (Constance Penley, *The Future of an Illusion* (1989))

Fantasy is a unique concept in psychoanalysis in referring to a psychic process that is both conscious and unconscious, and that juxtaposes the social and the psychic processes. (Elizabeth Cowie, 'Fantasia' (1990))

'What price the image of the woman?' Writing in 1979, Jacqueline Rose identifies that question as the legacy of feminism to psychoanalytic film theory. What feminism introduces into the psychoanalysis of film derived from Metz, Bellour, and Baudry is a conviction that the techniques of the imaginary, the resolutions of Oedipal narrative, and the totalising pleasures of the apparatus take place through an idea, and image, of the woman which remains occluded through these different theoretical approaches. Occluded in part because, as a range of feminist interventions has shown, the reference to sexual difference crucial to Freud's thinking has sometimes been lost in the move from psychoanalysis to film theory. 'Recent writing in *Screen* about psychoanalysis and cinema,' notes Laura Mulvey in her now classic 'Visual Pleasure and Narrative Cinema', 'has not sufficiently brought out the importance of the representation of the female form in a symbolic order in which, in the last resort, it speaks castration and nothing else' (Mulvey 1992: 22). The theme echoes through the work of, amongst others, Rose, Constance Penley, Elizabeth Cowie, Mary Ann Doane, Parveen Adams, and Joan Copjec. In so far as feminist film theory has been absorbed by the attempt to describe how and why the woman comes to bear the burden of the image of castration, it has pursued an account of sexual difference through the work of a number of psychoanalytic thinkers: Freud and Lacan, notably, but also Joan Riviere, Julia Kristeva, Luce Irigaray.

The range and diversity of that thinking emerges through the canonic essays of feminist film theory – essays that, in their different ways, will hark back to Freud's controversial analysis of sexual difference in a cluster of papers published between 1923 and 1933: 'The Infantile Genital Organization' (1923), 'The Dissolution of the Oedipus Complex' (1924), 'Some Psychical Consequences of the Anatomical Distinction Between the Sexes' (1925), 'Fetishism' (1927), 'Female Sexuality' (1931), 'Femininity' (1933). Crucial to the feminist reading (and, at times, repudiation) of psychoanalysis, these essays trace Freud's analysis of the feminine form of the Oedipus complex – an account of the woman as castrated 'bearer of the bleeding wound', as Mulvey summarises it (Mulvey 1992: 22).

As diverse as it is challenging, the reading that has taken place between psychoanalysis, feminism and cinema is characterised by a double movement. On the one hand, those theorists who bring psychoanalysis and feminism into the domain of cinema have complicated the idea of pleasure in image, in narrative, by turning to the concept of fantasy that, as we have seen, is never simply a question of pleasure for psychoanalysis. '*Why* does the subject necessarily seek only pleasure and its fulfilment?' asks Penley, faulting the theorists of the apparatus

(Metz, Baudry) for failing to take on the complexity of a psychoanalytic understanding of desire (the desire to have an unsatisfied desire, for example) (Penley 1989: 62). On the other hand, feminism has demonstrated the importance of extending the psychoanalytic frame of reference in film theory: tracking the concepts which have become central to that theory – imaginary, identification, disavowal, fetishism – back into psychoanalysis as well as broadening the range of psychoanalytic thinkers and texts brought to bear on film.[1]

Sexual difference and spectatorship

It would be difficult to imagine that work without Laura Mulvey's 'Visual Pleasure and Narrative Cinema', first published in the British film journal *Screen* in 1975. Part of a more general turn towards psychoanalysis which was taking place from within feminism – Juliet Mitchell's *Psychoanalysis and Feminism*, for example, was published in 1974 – Mulvey gave voice to a radical mistrust of pleasure which signalled a moment of anxiety and desire for *something else* in feminist film theory and practice. 'It is said,' Mulvey remarked, towards the beginning of 'Visual Pleasure', 'that analysing pleasure, or beauty, destroys it. That is the intention of this article'. It is an uncompromising statement of the politics – at once sexual and aesthetic – which sustain Mulvey's intervention; in particular, her drastic sexing of spectatorship which continues to haunt feminist engagements with film: 'Woman as Image, Man as Bearer of the Look. [...] The determining male gaze projects its phantasy on to the female figure which is styled accordingly'). It is in these terms that, as Mulvey was to put it some years later, her inaugural essay took on 'a life of its own' in the projects of feminist film theory (cited in Bergstrom and Doane 1989: vii).

As a film-maker, Mulvey would turn to the figure of the Sphinx – woman with the body of a beast, source of the enigma that drives Oedipus to his ruin – to explore the possibilities for a cinema able to counter the logic of image and narrative in Hollywood film.[2] Both her introduction and conclusion to 'Visual Pleasure' emphasise that alternative vision: the possibility of a break with a (Hollywood) film system grounded in masculine, and patriarchal, fantasies of the feminine. As a theorist of the visual, Mulvey turns to Freud and Lacan for the tools to psychoanalyse that fantasy of the woman. The scopophilic – voyeuristic, sadistic, fetishistic – child of Freud's essays on sexuality and sexual difference joins forces with Lacan's joyous mirror-baby to produce an account of the fascinations and identifications of cinema's imaginary. Freud's sketch of the encounter between boy and girl supposed to structure their different relations to the 'fact' of castration is remarkably invested. It is a sketch which founds sexual difference on an exchange of looks. The boy, gazing in horror at the 'mutilated creature' – the absence of a penis on the female body – is shocked into the belief that castration *can* happen; the girl, realising for the first time the extent of her own loss, is thrown into a state of consuming envy: 'She has seen it and knows that she is without it and wants to have it' (Freud 1925a: 252).

It is on the basis of this traumatised looking that Freud differentiates between masculine and feminine forms of the Oedipus complex. Identification with the law is, as we have seen, one route for the boy. Fetishism, the refusal to recognise the reality of the traumatic perception, is another. The fetish, Freud explains, is a form of protection against the threat of castration, a triumphant compromise. On the one hand, the little boy refuses to believe what he 'sees': the absence of the penis on a female (typically, the mother's) body. On the other hand, he does believe, creating the fetish through the force of what Freud describes as his 'counter-wish': the wish to find a penis on the female body is fulfilled through the fetish object (Freud 1927: 154). 'I know ... and I don't know' describes this special state of suspension of disbelief – a type of splitting of the ego that Freud will go on to describe as a form of disavowal (Freud 1940).

'I know ... and I don't know'; 'I know it's not true ... but all the same...' This, as Christian Metz is keen to argue, could be a description of the spectator, caught up in the impression of reality, the perceptual illusion – again, at once there and not there – of the cinema screen. 'Thus is established the lasting matrix,' Metz notes in a brief, but suggestive, discussion of disavowal towards the end of 'The Imaginary Signifier', 'the affective prototype of all the splittings of belief which man will henceforth be capable of in the most varied domains' (Metz 1982: 70). Including cinema. Believing and not believing, investing in the images of cinema as a form of prosthesis, the fetishist is a prototype of the spectator in cinema, fetishism the prototype of its pleasures. Only for the male spectator, Mulvey will insist. That is, the concepts of fetishism and disavowal that Metz wants to move into his theory of cinema only have meaning in psychoanalysis through a reference to the structure of sexual difference, a scene of traumatised looking. The argument runs through the feminist critique of apparatus theory.[3] 'In psychoanalytic terms,' Mulvey reiterates, 'the female figure ... connotes something that the look continually circles around but disavows: her lack of a penis, implying a threat of castration and hence unpleasure. Ultimately, the meaning of woman is sexual difference' (Mulvey 1992: 29).

It is from this point that Mulvey will introduce what Miriam Hansen has described as the 'classical choreography of the look' in feminist film theory (Hansen 1986: 11). The image of the woman on screen becomes the object of a 'masculine' look which identifies – more or less pleasurably, more or less omnipotently – with its like on screen:

As the spectator identifies with the main male protagonist, he projects his look on to that of his like, his screen surrogate, so that the power of the male protagonist as he controls events coincides with the active power of the erotic look, both giving a satisfying sense of omnipotence. (Mulvey 1992: 28)

By contrast, the female spectator is confronted with her image 'coded for strong visual and erotic impact', an image 'stolen' and made over to the demands of male fantasy. 'In a world ordered by sexual imbalance,' Mulvey clarifies, 'pleasure in looking has been split between active/male and passive/female' (27). That is, the pleasures of the imaginary – its fictions of agency and subjectivity – are not there for the woman who appears in the mirror only in the name of someone else's fantasy. It is a type of visible invisibility – a being there without being there – which has had a determining influence on feminist film theory. 'What was so overwhelmingly recognisable in "Visual Pleasure",' note Janet Bergstrom and Mary Ann Doane in their reflections on Mulvey's essay for 'The Spectatrix', 'was our own absence' – an absence which generates one of the founding questions of feminist film theory: 'What about the female spectator?' (Bergstrom and Doane 1989: 7).

On the one hand, the force of Mulvey's argument is its refusal to give way on the relation between sex and spectatorship – a spectatorship that exceeds the specific instance of cinema.[4] By keeping the idea of a 'world ordered by sexual imbalance' in her sights, Mulvey pulls film theory towards feminist discussions of the position of women in culture – pulls film theory towards the world, as it were. On the other hand, her sexing of the looking, and pleasure, of cinema opened up the space in feminist film theory for an apparently interminable analysis of the dilemmas of the female spectator. Itself a monument to that overly familiar figure, 'The Spectatrix' (a special issue of the influential journal of feminism and film, *Camera Obscura*) included four surveys and over fifty individual responses to a questionnaire drafted by Bergstrom and Doane. As Jackie Stacey summarised the problem, the female spectator has been offered (by cinema, by theory) the 'three rather frustrating options of masculinisation, masochism or marginality': she can look 'as a man'; she can take pleasure in, and identify with, her own objectification and alienation in the image; or, she can take on – with anxiety or pleasure, or both – her position on the outside of patriarchal fantasy (Stacey 1987: 51).

What place for the desire of the woman in a structure dominated by (masculine) voyeurism and fetishism? The female spectator, at once identifying and dissociated (a type of hysteric?), represents an impasse for a feminist approach to film that has been caught up in the attempt to theorise the relation between spectator and screen.[5] Oscillating between the debasement of the image of the feminine and the illusory mastery of the masculine ego, there has been a tendency in feminist discussion of spectatorship to reinforce an equation between identification and (narcissistic) recognition of the self in the image on screen. Against this, feminist film scholars have explored more complex, and less gendered, models of fantasy and identification in cinema. In particular, Elizabeth Cowie's analysis of Irving Rapper's *Now Voyager* (1942) in 'Fantasia', published in *m/f* in 1984, is a key intervention in the field. Setting out the historical and theoretical contexts in which feminist analyses of sexuality and cinema were taking place at the beginning of the 1980s, Cowie offered a reading of Freud's papers on creativity and daydreaming through the work of Jean Laplanche and Jean-Bertrand Pontalis (notably, their influential 'Fantasy and the Origins of Sexuality' (1986)). At issue is the idea of fantasy as a *'mise-en-scène* of desire,' as Cowie recalls in 'The Spectatrix', 'which can be seen to have multiple places for the subject of the fantasy, and for the viewing subject who, through identification, may similarly take up these multiple positions' (Bergstrom and Doane 1989: 129). In other words, the articulation between desire and identification can be understood not only in terms of the subject's relation to an object (the Oedipal desire for the mother that, on one reading, casts the subject as masculine) but as a process of setting, or staging – a *mise-en-scène* in which the subject plays with, and inserts herself into, a sequence of narrative and images. That play may be read in terms of wishing and anxiety, pleasure and defence, voyeurism and fetishism. But it does not tie the subject to *one* identity, one *place* in the story. 'These are not simple alternatives,' Cowie insists, in the course of a discussion of the complex construction of sexual difference through the image and narrative of the film text. 'Furthermore, these positions are not fixed by or dependent upon the gender of either characters or the spectator'.

The appeal of Cowie's approach is its strong sense of the female spectator as a concept which rests on the cusp between the construc-tions of sexual difference in cinema and the lived effects of that differ-ence for women in a society bound to the norms of gender identity. Films, on Cowie's readings, are forms of public fantasy – fantasy which both protests against and conforms to the conventions of sexuality and sexual difference. *Now Voyager*, for instance, exemplifies the wishfulfilment of Hollywood cinema, the ready-made formula of family and romance (a version of Heath's family machine). In the transformation of Charlotte Vale (Bette Davis) from ugly duckling to society beauty, from persecuted spinster-daughter to object of erotic desire, Cowie suggests, Rapping's melodrama engages a series of ambitious and erotic wishes familiar to the point of banality. At the same time, there is a twist to this well-known tale which ends, Cowie recalls, with 'an apparently unfulfilled wish' (Adams and Cowie 1990: 176). Because Jerry (married to an ailing wife) and Charlotte cannot marry, their love remains unacknowledged by the world; but Charlotte wins Tina, Jerry's daughter, in his place – the child who she promises to love and bring up as her own. In other words, this is an Oedipal narrative, but one with a twist: the daughter fulfils the wish to have a child by 'evict[ing] the father', and thereby setting herself up as 'the "good" mother against Mrs. Vale's "bad" mother' (177). That is, on Cowie's reading, a 'homosexual desire [is] played across the film': on the one hand, the bond between (substitute) mother and daughter is fundamental to the passion, and pleasure, of the film; on the other hand, Charlotte is cast as a 'phallic' mother: the woman who does not lack, who has her relation with a child without reference to a husband/father. 'This is not Charlotte's fantasy,' Cowie explains towards the end of her reading of the film, 'but the "film's" fantasy. It is an effect of its narration (of its *énonciation*)' (178).

That reference to its *énonciation* – not *what* the film says but how it says it and to whom – reinforces the idea of film as a form of address, a staging of desire which presents not one (Oedipal) trajectory but various scenarios which, Cowie concludes, 'are not only successive, but also compounded, each containing elements of the others' (177). As a form of public wishfulfilment, then, cinema requires not 'universal objects of desire, but a setting of desiring in which we find our place(s)' (168). *Finding* his or her place, the spectator is engaged in and by that wishing, both mobile and fixed. 'Subject-positions shift across the boundary of sexual difference,' as Cowie puts it, 'but do so always in terms of sexual difference' (195). Sexual difference, it seems, is the fantasy that refuses to give way – a refusal which is both the strength, and the felt restriction, of psychoanalytic feminist theory. Ellen Seiter, amongst others, makes the point forcefully in her contribution to 'The Spectatrix': 'I think that psychoanalytic theory has blinded feminist film studies to the significance of race and class difference. This is why theoretical work on the female spectator may have reached a dead end' (Bergstrom and Doane 1989: 283).

The charge returns, over and over again, to psychoanalysis and to psychoanalytic studies of culture. So far as feminist film theory is concerned, it is a charge which needs to be tested against one of its most pervasive, and troubling, concepts of femininity and female spectatorship – a concept which forms a bridge between feminist perspectives on the idea of difference and those associated with queer, postcolonial and black literary/cultural studies. Once again, coming in response to the question of how the woman might look and identify in cinema, the publication in *Screen* in 1982 of Mary Ann Doane's (frequently anthologised) essay, 'Film and the Masquerade: Theorising the Female Spectator' imported into film theory one of the most significant contributions to the psychoanalysis of femininity and female sexuality: Joan Riviere's 'Womanliness as a Masquerade', first published in *The International Journal of Psychoanalysis* in 1929.[6] It is an essay that, as Jean Walton has recently pointed out, induced a critical silence concerning the 'explicit delineation of racial difference' in the concept of the masquerade (Walton 1995: 781). In other words, 'Womanliness as a Masquerade' brings right to the fore the problem for feminist film theory of how to think about the *difference* of sexual difference – the relation between feminism and other discourses of, or on, difference which is now central to psychoanalytic studies in film.

Womanliness as a Masquerade

Translator of Freud and early follower of Melanie Klein, Joan Riviere is a distinguished figure in the history of psychoanalysis. Outside of the psychoanalytic institution, she is known (almost) solely through her account of femininity in 'Womanliness as a Masquerade'.[7] As Lisa Appignanesi and John Forrester put it in their invaluable study of *Freud's*

Women in 1992, in this essay Riviere introduced 'a feminine character far more resonant with contemporary experience than any Freud or even Helene Deutsch had explored. Her subject is the intellectual woman – a subject, given herself and the high proportion of women in the British Society, which she knew well' (Appignanesi and Forrester 1992: 363). Similarly, in his commentary on Riviere's masquerade (published alongside her essay in *Formations of Fantasy*) Stephen Heath suggested that to read the terms in which Ernest Jones (Riviere's first analyst) presents her to Freud – as a woman demonstrating 'typical hysteria', 'sexual anaesthesia', 'masculine identification' – is to 'find oneself at once in the world of her "Masquerade" paper. [...] Relations between the paper and the life are doubtless strong, more than strong' (Heath 1986: 46).

'Womanliness as a Masquerade' is Riviere's contribution to the 'great debate' on female sexuality that took place in psychoanalysis during the late 1920s and 1930s. A variety of contributions from, amongst others, Ernest Jones, Karen Horney, Helene Deutsch, and Melanie Klein fed into the debate on the identity of femininity: crudely, is it an essence (preceding the law, preceding any complex) or a difference (a different relation to the law, a difference from the masculine – which is then set up as norm)? Turning on the question of the castration complex, it was a debate that divided psychoanalysts. 'The issue was posed as the nature of female sexuality,' writes Juliet Mitchell in her introduction to the topic in 1982, 'but underlying that were the preceding disagreements on castration anxiety' (Mitchell and Rose 1982: 7).

In other words, the 'great debate' (Lacan would call it a war) returns feminism and film theory to the scene of traumatised looking from which Freud derives his analysis of sexual difference and the Oedipus complex (more precisely, the Oedipus complex as the structuring of sexual difference). It is a decisive scene in which, as we have seen, the visual is reduced to the perceptual: castration becomes a 'sight' in which the girl carries the burden of deficiency: 'nothing to be seen as having nothing', as Rose puts it (Rose 1986: 202). On this model, the threat of castration can have no meaning for the girl: quite simply, she has 'nothing to lose'. 'In the absence of fear of castration,' Freud explains, carefully,

> the chief motive is lacking which leads boys to surmount the Oedipus complex. Girls remain in it for an indeterminate length of time; they demolish it late and, even so, incompletely. In these circumstances the formation of the super-ego must suffer: it cannot attain the strength and independence which give it its cultural significance, and feminists are not pleased when we point out to them the effects of this factor upon the average feminine character. (Freud 1933: 129)

Certainly, feminists were not pleased to hear Freud's bleak account of women's character: 'weaker in their social interests' than men, he insists, women have less sense of justice, less tolerance of law, suffer more from the effects of an overweening envy (134). In the classic Freudian schema, what the girl lacks above all is a reason to obey the profoundly socialising law against incest. The lack that marks her sexual difference determines her relation to an Oedipal fantasy which has been used to denote the formation of modern cultural life. The feminine exists at the point of failure, a falling outside of the law of the father that, on one feminist reading, can be recast as a source of resistance. 'The fact that women are "weaker in their social interests",' retorts Luce Irigaray, 'is obvious ... [in] a society in which they have no stake' (Irigaray 1985: 119). In this case, the re-elaboration of the symbolic in order to open up a space for the feminine becomes central to the feminist political project – a type of thinking, or imagining for the future. In terms of cinema, studies of the 'woman's film' of the 1940s, of women's 'friendship films', as well as films made by women, have contributed to that imagining.[8] But for feminist film theory to exploit the purchase, as well as the difficulty, of Freud's account of the feminine Oedipus complex, it must keep in mind that suffering of the feminine superego. Freud's account of femininity and female sexuality can be (and has been) challenged. But it does maintain a concept of the feminine which is inseparable from the process by which the subject invests itself in the world: that is, a concept of femininity which cannot be reduced to an essence, which cannot be thought outside of the structures – psychical, social, cultural – which form our experience of reality. Femininity is *both* a sexual and a social category; that is, sexual difference has no meaning for Freud outside of a differentiated relation to the Oedipal law which routes the child into (or out of) collective life.

In other words, the sexually 'mutilated' body of the woman symbolises a disturbance at the level of the subject's investiture in the formations of culture. (In film theory, that disturbance goes by the name of the female spectator.) But it is Freud's insight into a disturbance which passes from sexual to social – or makes the social and sexual implicit to one another – which can be brought to bear on feminist uses of Riviere's concept of masquerade. It is well-known that Riviere based her account of the masquerade on the analysis of a successful, intellectual American woman 'engaged in work of a propagandist nature which consisted principally in speaking and writing' (Riviere 1986: 36). Suffering from feelings of acute anxiety after every public performance, Riviere notes, this patient was compelled to 'seek some attention or complimentary notice from a man or men at the close of the proceedings in which she had taken part or been the principal figure'. Her symptom took the form of a 'compulsive ogling and coquetting' that Riviere explains as a form of defence: the defensive mask of femininity. The exhibition in public of the woman's intellectual gifts, Riviere insists,

> signified an exhibition of herself in possession of the father's penis, having castrated him. The display once over, she was seized by horrible dread of the retribution the father would then exact. Obviously it was a step towards propitiating the avenger to endeavour to offer herself to him sexually. (37)

For Riviere, the woman's compulsive flirtation with a man or men in her audience is a version of another (unconscious) scene of robbing and despoiling the father, a scene which finds its purchase in the mismatch between the socio-cultural norm of the feminine – passive, private – and the public, or 'masculine', persona assumed by the patient in her professional life. It is *after* she has worn the mask of masculinity that the woman takes refuge in the masquerade of an appeasing womanliness.[9] In this sense, the male spectators listening to and looking at the woman's performance have to be understood as (daytime) substitutes for the castrated father of unconscious fantasy. At the same time, the aim of the 'compulsive reversal of her intellectual performance', Riviere continues, is not only to evoke 'friendly feelings towards her in the man' but 'to make sure of safety by masquerading as guiltless and innocent'. In other words, femininity is staged as a sign of guiltlessness, the sign that a crime (robbery, castration) has not taken place. The two together (the public performance, its obsessive undoing) are then mapped onto the woman's incessant oscillation between masculinity and femininity – an oscillation which prompts Riviere's celebrated statement of the indistinction between womanliness and the masquerade:

The reader may now ask how I define womanliness or where I draw the line between genuine womanliness and the 'masquerade'. My suggestion is not, however, that there is any such difference; whether radical or superficial, they are the same thing. The capacity for womanliness was there in this woman [but] was used far more as a device for avoiding anxiety than as a primary mode of sexual enjoyment. (38)

Once again, what both psychoanalysis and feminism confront in this passage is a hesitation between an essential sexuality which is always, in the last instance, able to be put in its place ('genuine womanliness' as a capacity belonging to all women) and a way of thinking about identity as something more like a technique, a 'device' to be used – towards pleasure, say, or against anxiety. There is an enormous tension in Riviere's essay between a womanliness that, like the clothing to which it is so often compared, can be put on and off at will, and femininity as a primary mode of being (sexual) for the woman. Far from resolving that tension, Riviere appears to embrace it ('My suggestion is not, however, that there is any such difference'). For a feminism which puts the emphasis on the idea of femininity as a demand imposed by masculine, or patriarchal, structures of desire, it is easy to see the visual convention of the masquerade as a sign of the woman's alienation from herself and her own desire. Ultimately recoverable, both self and desire can become the quest of feminism, the elusive objects sustaining its project. On the other hand, as spectacle of sexual mobility, the masquerade can become the distinguishing feature of a femininity which signals the impossibility of achieving, or knowing, the identity of either sex, male or female. 'Femininity,' as Mary Ann Doane puts it in her essay on the theme, 'is constructed as mask – as the decorative layer which conceals non-identity' (Doane 2000: 502). Marked by its production of an excessive – quasi-parodic, flaunting – femininity, the masquerade offers a form of resistance to what Doane describes as a masculine fantasy in which the woman is (over)identified with her image: that image-to-be-looked-at which is the focus of Mulvey's 'Visual Pleasure'. 'The effectivity of masquerade,' Doane concludes, 'lies precisely in its potential to manufacture a distance from the image, to generate a problematic within which the image is manipulable, producible, and readable by the woman' (507).

Clearly, the masquerade can become a potent force for a feminist film theory that has taken over Doane's emphasis on femininity as a spectacle of sexual oscillation and pretence. So often equated with the idea of a copy for which there is no original, with non-identity – 'sexual mobility would seem to be a distinguishing feature of femininity in its cultural construction', as Doane puts it – the masquerade coincides with a Lacanian investment in identity as fabrication, fiction, *fantasy* (502). In particular, the idea of the woman – of femininity, feminine sexuality – as a fantasy comes through the influential collection of Lacan's papers, *Feminine Sexuality – Jacques Lacan and the École freudienne*, edited by Juliet Mitchell and Jacqueline Rose in 1982. Keeping his sights on the relation between sexuality and the unconscious, Lacan intervenes in the 'great debate' by shifting its terms: if the unconscious is a site of division of the subject from him or herself (a division that we saw played out in relation to the mirror stage, for example), then the idea of sexuality as an essence, as part of a single *identity*, is misplaced from the start. What Freud discovers in the Oedipus complex (including its reference to castration), Lacan insists, is that (sexual) identity is taken on 'by means of a threat' (Mitchell and Rose 1982: 75). It is a threat which speaks to the force, and anxiety, involved in what Lacan wants to describe as 'not a contingent, but an essential disturbance of human sexuality'.

On this reading, both castration anxiety and its equally controversial counterpart, penis envy, are signs of that disturbance: the effects of the Oedipal structure through which the child takes up a sexed position as male or female. The price of that position, Lacan maintains, is a persistent sense that something is missing – a sense of loss that he will attempt to explain by making the connection between the unconscious, sexuality and symbolisation.

Let us recall Freud's hallucinating baby – the infant who conjures an hallucinatory image in the place of the (memory of the) breast. First wish, first fantasy, first symbolisation: the baby is masking a lack – the sense of something missing – with an image. Later, language – words that fill an empty mouth, as the psychoanalysts Nicolas Abraham and Maria Torok describe it – will take up the challenge, helping us to forge an identity premised on, and covering over, that first experience of loss (Abraham and Torok 1994: 127). 'Language speaks the loss which lay behind that first moment of symbolisation,' Rose writes in her introduction to *Feminine Sexuality*. 'When the child asks something of its mother, that loss will persist over and above anything which she can possibly give, or say, in reply' (Mitchell and Rose 1982: 32). It is on the basis of this persistent loss that Lacan will introduce his influential (and sometimes elusive) distinction between demand and desire. While demand may aim at something that (in principle) could be given or withheld, it also 'bears on something other than the satisfactions which it calls for': that is, on the realm of desire born out of that primordial experience of lack, desire as the desire for an 'impossible' object: the object that does not, and cannot, exist (80).

For a fantasmatic object, precisely. For Lacan, this is the phallus and the work of taking up a sexed identity (male or female) is that of taking up a position in relation to the phallus. It is in this sense, too, that Lacanian theorists can begin to speak of the woman as a fantasy for both men and women. In particular, the idea of male and female, masculine and feminine, as coherent and complementary to one another is *the* fantasy of sexual love (a fantasy trafficked by cinema and, Lacan would add, some forms of psychoanalysis). Image of castration, the woman carries the burden of incompleteness, of something missing; object of desire, she promises completion, the coherence – imaginary, idealised – of the couple. Nothing missing. In other words, she is a type of fetish.

It is the Lacanian version of Riviere's essay that echoes through feminist film theory.[10] The idea of woman as fantasy, of feminine identity as destabilised, even playful, has overshadowed her essay and, notably, the emphasis on threat that Riviere shares with Lacan. In particular, the idea of the masquerade as a strategy of appeasement – an attempt to ward off the vengeance that, at the level of unconscious fantasy, the woman expects from the father – has come into film theory cut off from the material which surrounds it. The key passage, which comes just before Riviere's conclusion concerning the indistinction between femininity and masquerade, reads as follows:

> The exhibition in public of her intellectual proficiency, which was in itself carried through successfully, signified an exhibition of herself in possession of her father's penis, having castrated him. The display once over, she was seized by a horrible dread of the retribution the father would then exact. Obviously it was a step towards propitiating the avenger to endeavour to offer herself to him sexually [the 'compulsive ogling and coquetting']. This phantasy, it then appeared, had been very common in her childhood and youth, which had been spent in the Southern States of America; if a negro came to attack her, she planned to defend herself by making him kiss her and make love to her (ultimately so that she could then deliver him over to justice). But there was a

further determinant of the obsessive behaviour. In a dream which had a rather similar content to this childhood phantasy, she was in terror alone in the house; then a negro came in and found her washing clothes, with her sleeves rolled up and arms exposed. She resisted him, with the secret intention of attracting him sexually, and he began to admire her arms and caress them and her breasts. The meaning was that she had killed father and mother and obtained everything for herself (alone in the house), became terrified of their retribution (expected shots through the window), and defended herself by taking on a menial role (washing clothes) and by *washing off* dirt and sweat, guilt and blood, everything she had obtained by the deed, and "disguising herself" as merely a castrated woman. In that guise, the man found no stolen property on her which he need attack her to recover and, further, found her attractive as an object of love. Thus the aim of the compulsion was not merely to secure reassurance by evoking friendly feelings towards her in the man; it was chiefly to make sure of safety by masquerading as guiltless and innocent.

Before this dream she had had dreams of people putting masks on their faces in order to avert disaster. One of these dreams was of a high tower on a hill being pushed over and falling down on the inhabitants of a village below, but the people put on masks and escaped injury! (Riviere 1986: 37-8)

One of the most striking aspects of this passage is the way in which it seems to confirm, almost parodically, the two prevalent accusations against psychoanalysis: first, that psychoanalysis always loses sight of, and so seduces its readers into losing sight of, the domains of culture and politics; secondly, that its readings perform a hermeneutic reduction in their relentless imposition onto diverse forms of psychical and cultural material of an Oedipal/familial paradigm.[11] Almost compulsively, Riviere derives both the woman's symptom, as well as her fantasies and dreams, from the unconscious fantasy of having castrated her father. Her patient's 'compulsive ogling and coquetting', her childhood fantasy of being attacked by and then seducing a black man and, finally, her dream of resisting a black man in the hope of seducing him are all brought back to an original scene of robbery and attack against the father, or the father's penis. In this sense, it is as if the three different forms of representation mentioned by Riviere (symptom, childhood phantasy, dream) are reduced to a single, concealed content. Thus Riviere can locate the daydream of being attacked by a black man between the symptom and the unconscious fantasy; she can set up a relation of substitution or displacement – familiar from Freud's account of *The Interpretation of Dreams* – between the robbed father of unconscious fantasy, the 'real' men in the audience and the black man who can only have come to attack her.

On Riviere's account, the link between these figures is the woman's attempt to defend herself from their vengeance by making herself sexually attractive to them. But in order to make this interpretation, she has to bracket an element of what she tells us of her patient's fantasy: 'If a negro came to attack her, she planned to defend herself by making him kiss her and make to love to her (ultimately so that she could then deliver him over to justice)'. We can open up this parenthesis on to a number of different readings. In the first place, Riviere's use of parenthesis suggests the pressure of disguise or censorship within the psychoanalytic narrative itself – a force of distortion on the inside of the very statement which offers to clarify and explain. That censorship is then repeated through Riviere's narrative in the form of a repression of precisely that element of the woman's fantasy life which seems both to disrupt the substitution of the father of unconscious fantasy for the black man and to embed a specific social and historical context in the fantasy itself. More specifically, as the woman's appeal to justice begins to make clear, she is disguising herself as innocent and seductive not only so that she can make herself 'attractive as an object of love', as Riviere puts it, but also to elaborate the fiction of a retributive justice against those who threaten to attack her. That fiction is both displayed, and masked, by Riviere who, when she isolates and ignores her patient's fantasmatic appeal to the law, begins to destroy the connection made between the fantasy of being attacked by a black man and this woman's desire for justice. In other words, in her published version of the case, Riviere does not read the aggressive desire for vengeance which shows up through this patient's apparent fantasy of appeasement – an aggression which identifies the woman's desire *with* that of the vengeful father of unconscious fantasy.

Riviere both does, and does not, acknowledge this aggression. Her careful, but unelaborated, location of her patient's childhood in the Southern States of America – presumably during the late nineteenth or early twentieth century – raises the question of the relation between the woman's childhood fantasies and the race politics of the American South.

The parallels between the fantasies supporting the masquerade and what Jacqueline Dowd Hall has described as the sexual imaginary of the Southern States are obvious. In her history of Jessie Daniel Ames and the Women's Campaign Against Lynching, for example, Hall writes of one 'turn of the century' woman for whom the South had become 'a smouldering volcano, the dark of its quivering night ... pierced through by the cry of some outraged woman' (Dowd Hall 1983: 341). Compare George T. Winston: 'The southern woman and her helpless little children in a solitary farm house no longer sleeps secure. [...] The black brute is lurking in the dark' (344).

As Hall goes on to suggest, the web of connections between racist and sexual ideologies in the South bound the purity (guiltlessness) and honour of the white Southern woman to the killing of black men. Men who lived under what Alice Walker has described as the slander that 'where white women are concerned, [they] are creatures of uncontrollable lust' (Walker 1986: 94). The effects of that slander, and of the imaginary which subtends it, is confirmed by Dowd Hall: 'Even as white moderates criticised lynching in the abstract, they continued [in the 1920s and 1930s] to justify outbreaks of mob violence for the one special crime of sexual assault' (Dowd Hall 1983: 344).

It is her patient's reference to that 'special crime' which embeds the spectacle of lynching in Riviere's analysis of the feminine masquerade.[12]

Consider Dowd Hall's summary version of the persecutory scene that turns the white woman into victimised spectator of her own revenge:

> The frail victim, leaning on the arms of her male relatives, might be brought to the scene of the crime, there to identify her assailant and witness his execution. This was a moment of humiliation. A woman who had just been raped, or who had been apprehended in a clandestine interracial affair, or whose male relatives were pretending that she had been raped, stood on display before the whole community. (343)

Such a scene is also, as David Marriott has pointed out recently, a scene of desire: a spectacle of (black) annihilation and (white) appetite for murder which turns law into terror (Marriott 2000: 1-22). 'If this is law,' Marriott suggests (troping Richard Wright's maxim: 'the law is white'), 'it is both fantasmatic and perverse' (6). The narratives and images of lynching explored by Marriott – in particular, his analysis of lynching as spectacle to be photographed – restores the violence which goes missing in both Riviere's and film theory's account of the masquerade. More precisely, his disturbing account of the bloody rituals of lynching suggest that the ferocity of unconscious life taken for granted by Riviere has been transferred to the outside world, taken on by a community that through the torture and destruction of black bodies mimes the violence of the parental imagos which mutilate, devour, castrate, and kill – in fantasy (Riviere 1986: 41). Marriott cites the testimony given by Howard Kester in *The Lynching of Claude Neal* in 1934: 'After taking the nigger to the woods ... they cut off his penis. He was made to eat it. Then they cut off his testicles and made him eat them and say he liked it'). 'To hear him desire his own death,' Marriott concludes in his interpretation of this by no means uncommon incident, ' – and so turn their terrible pleasure into his own violent wish – was to construct a vision of the castrated black man as one actively seeking the pleasures of castration' (6-9).

Alternatively: what Riviere has recorded in 'Womanliness as a Masquerade' is a fantasy at the juncture between unconscious and cultural forms of violence (another way of thinking about the 'typical dream'). Drawing attention to the presence of the woman's male kin in the scene of accusation and retribution central to what she describes as the Southern white rape complex, Dowd Hall points to the fact that this fantasy is fabricated not only by and for the woman in question but for the culture – as racist as it is patriarchal – in which she takes up her part. That is, the masquerade is elaborated on behalf of the woman, certainly, but also with another gaze in view – what Slavoj Žižek might call the symbolic, or paternal, gaze. In fact, Žižek's analysis of hysteria – the hysterical body with which we began and to which the masquerade is so frequently compared – can be mapped onto the fantasm of sexuality and destruction at the heart of Riviere's essay. 'Behind an extremely "feminine" imaginary figure,' he writes in *The Sublime Object of Ideology*, 'we can thus generally discover some kind of masculine, paternal identification: she is enacting fragile femininity, but on the symbolic level she is in fact identified with the paternal gaze, to which she wants to appear likeable' (Žižek 1989: 106).

Gaze/image: the distinction may offer a way out of the impasse (a 'kind of ennui' as Bergstrom and Doane put it in 'The Spectatrix') at the heart of feminist film theory (Bergstrom and Doane 1989: 15). Certainly, it seems to answer the double demand made by film scholars on psychoanalysis for a theory of identification in cinema as the site of both fantasmatic mobility – various, and unpredictable, play with a sequence of narrative and images – *and* fixation (the recurrence of the Oedipal structure in Hollywood film, say, or its typical dreams of sex and race). It is that fixation which re-inflects the masquerade of womanliness as a death threat – a threat, a *history*, which becomes more apparent if we insist on the Oedipal dynamic supporting Riviere's analysis of the masquerade as an unconscious scenario of paternal appeasement. It may be that, as fantasy, the substitution of the black man for the paternal imago allows the woman to continue her attack against the father; that is, the black man veils her attack against the father and his precious possession. But as fantasy *and* real event the black male body pays the price. Lift Riviere's repression of the woman's stated desire for justice, and the figure of the black man is cast not only as object of desire and threat, but as a legitimate object of persecution. The black man is not only a substitute for the father of unconscious fantasy, but a burned and hanged offering to him.

Cinema: technique of aggression?

What does cinema have to do with the racism that supports Riviere's concept of the masquerade? The racist symbolics of the American South had recently been re-run in one of the foundational texts of narrative film: D.W. Griffith's *Birth of a Nation* (1915) – a cinematic vision of 'the black peril' as Harry A. Potamkin was to put it also in 1929 (Donald *et al.* 1998: 70). A film which 'employed the old rape idea', in Geraldyn Dismond's phrase, to tell the history of the aftermath of the American Civil War through the story of two families: the Camerons, representatives of the Old South, and the Stonemans, the Northerners (74). As its advertising campaign made so apparent, the Ku Klux Klan were the heroes of Griffith's film in which, as Mary Ann Doane has pointed out, 'the white woman is the stake of a virulent racism' (Doane 1991: 228; Maltby 1995). In this sense, the vision of white femininity – helpless, pure, under siege – travels between *Birth of a Nation* and 'Womanliness as a Masquerade', becoming part of the circulation, and recombination, of terms in a fantasm which cannot be contained as either 'cinema' or 'psychoanalysis'. 'The number of lynchings of African-Americans by white mobs,' notes Richard Maltby, 'increased dramatically in the few years after [the film's] release' (Maltby 1995: 365).

Reading across from Griffith's film to Riviere's speculations on the mask, each text appears to give voice and image to what remains unsaid and unseen in the other. In its overt racism, for example, *Birth of a Nation* displays the connection between that hyperbolic femininity (Doane draws attention to the photograph of Elsie Stoneman which circulates through the film) and a stereotypical image of the black man as sexual aggressor and/or passive victim – images that remain staples of Hollywood film. By contrast, Riviere's attention to the anxiety and subterfuge involved in her patient's 'femaleness' uncovers the tension internal to the assumption of that stereotype, of (sexual) identity as such – identity that, as Rose puts it, is 'neither simply achieved nor ever complete' (Rose 1986: 7). It is in this context that *Birth of a Nation* and 'Womanliness as a Masquerade' converge in their discovery, and deployment, of sexualised and racialised formations of narrative and spectacle. The place of *Birth of a Nation* in American film history is secure, if controversial, with critical debate often trenched on how far Griffith's formal innovations in film narrative can be separated from the trade in racist stereotypes. Similarly, while it is difficult to maintain the concept of masquerade as a strategy for feminist resistance to the voyeurism of cinema, Riviere's essay is a crucial point of contact between feminist film theory and the psychoanalysis of racism which has been taking place through the work of, amongst others, Gwen Bergner, Homi Bhabha, Stuart Hall, David Marriott, and Kobena Mercer.[13]

Coming in the wake of Frantz Fanon's *Black Skin, White Masks* (1952) – a book that, in its exploration of the black man as object of a phobic *look*, shares the rhetoric of masking – that work brings the question of racism and cinema into dialogue with a psychoanalysis of hatred: the imaginary, and stereotypical, vision of the black as phobic object of European and Anglo-American cultures. Taking Lacan's theory of the imaginary as one of the starting-points for his own thinking on identification – in literature, in cinema, in culture – Fanon cues a reading of racism in terms of the libidinal rivalries of the mirror stage, the images and narratives which sustain the work of individual and cultural identity. In fact, *Black Skin, White Masks* is one of the first uses of the mirror stage as a means to cultural critique. 'But when we say,' Fanon insists, 'that European culture possesses an *imago* of the negro responsible for all the conflicts that may arise, we do not go beyond the real' (Fanon 1986: 169; translation slightly modified). In saying this, Fanon is not only staking a claim to the truth-value of his analysis but also uncovering a fantasmatic image of the black man structuring the reality – the real conflict, the racist violence – of European and Anglo-American cultures. The force, and the difficulty, of Fanon's psychoanalysis derives from that doubling of his critical focus: *Black Skin, White Masks* presents an analysis of the black man, of blackness, as a fantasy, but a fantasy that is also a real event – a presence in and a pressure on the real.[14] At the same time, as critics are now beginning to explore, Fanon's analysis of the figure of blackness is inseparable from his response to cinema. On Marriott's view, for example, *Black Skin, White Masks* is a book which 'returns insistently, even symptomatically, to images of black men – and black soldiers – in mainstream American cinema' (Marriott 2000: 67-8). In her contribution to a recent collection on Fanon, E. Ann Kaplan tracks the idea of cinema as trauma through *Black Skin, White Masks*: 'I am interested in how Fanon's trauma of race is worked through both his body and his responses to American cinema in *Black Skin, White Masks*' (Kaplan 1999: 150). In his turn to the mirror stage to think through these issues, then, Fanon takes his readers back to the analysis of cinema as a technique of the imaginary – but one in which the question of aggression is brought right to the fore.[15]

The question is at the origins of feminist film theory, but it remains more or less occluded through the discussions of fantasy and spectatorship explored in this chapter. It is as if the tangled relations among masculinity, looking and aggression have pulled feminist film theory away from a consideration of aggression as that which belongs not to one of the terms in a pair of oppositions (to the masculine as opposed to the feminine, say) but to the alternation between the two. The point was made as early as 1976 when, in a return to Bellour's analysis of the Bodega Bay sequence of *The Birds*, Jacqueline Rose drew attention to the instability and aggression written into the concept of the imaginary – the concept that, as we have seen, was dominating discussion of the idea of cinema as apparatus.[16] On the one hand, it is her attention to the place of the woman at the level of narrative as well as spectacle which sustains Rose's account of what she describes as the paranoid mechanism of Hitchcock's film: crudely, its success in externalising the fear of attack which is one aspect of Lacan's analysis of the self-objectifying identification which founds the ego (see Chapter 2). On the other hand, at issue is the possibility that aggression does not belong to the 'male' look as such, but to the alternation between the subject seeing and the subject seen (that is, to the alternation between masculine and feminine, to *sexual difference*). 'Aggressivity is a function of the alternation,' Rose concludes, and not derived from one of its terms' (93). Paranoia belongs to the fact that the seeing subject (the spectator) may be the object of a persecutory look that becomes known only at the moment of assault. To push the point, both Oedipal narrative and imaginary apparatus cohere (in so far as they do) by finding *someone* to bear the burden of the splitting of the subject in the mirror stage – the aggressivity unleashed at the very moment of fabricating identity. That is, if cinema is a technique of the imaginary, then it is also, necessarily, a technique of aggression.

The insight remains to be explored, but it recasts the question that opened this chapter. What price the image? Part of the legacy of psychoanalysis to feminism, the difficulty persists. As an account of subjectivity that is always, and necessarily, divided, psychoanalysis troubles the fantasy of identity and coherence – including the fantasy of looking *as* a woman, identifying *as* a woman in cinema. Who pays the price of the fantasy of identity and coherence? (Or, indeed, of its inverse: the play of masquerade and fragmentation?) On the cusp between feminism and Black Cultural Studies, psychoanalytic film theory may be able to (re-)open the question – beyond the impasse of the female spectator.

CONCLUSION

What now for psychoanalysis and cinema? Part of the work involved in writing – and, I hope, in reading – this book was that of re-discovering how
preoccupying the question could be. While the exchange between psychoanalysis and cinema can be focused through the psychoanalytic film theory
that has been the primary subject of this book, there are other points of
convergence emerging in some of the most recent scholarship in film.

On the one hand, for example, the relation between psychoanalysis and
cinema is being explored increasingly in terms of their shared history –
the 'symbiotic relationship' between the two as Laura Marcus puts it in
her invaluable commentaries on the early film journal, *Close Up* (Donald *et
al.* 1998: 240). In the early decades of the twentieth century, that history
may well be inseparable from the ventures of literary modernism (Marcus
focuses on the writings of both Dorothy Richardson and the American poet
and film-maker, H.D., who entered into analysis with Freud at the beginning of the 1930s). In this context, too, the concepts of shock and trauma
central to the representation of the modern in both literature and cinema
can become a new point of contact with psychoanalysis – *its* engagement
with the vicissitudes of trauma and pleasure in symptom, in dream and in
fantasy.

In fact, Freud's attention to the experience of shock, his discovery of
the 'talking cure' as a means to *process* the effects of shock, casts psychoanalysis as a modern technology of self – one that runs parallel with cinema

as another new technology of modernity. That parallelism is helping to sustain a new sense of pluralism in the study of cinema and psychoanalysis; in particular, a wish to provide a forum in which psychoanalysts and film scholars can meet and exchange views. But, as Janet Bergstrom notes in her introduction to a recent volume of essays collected with precisely that aim in view: 'Dialogue between constituencies seem[s] blocked to a surprising degree' (Bergstrom 1999: 1).

Blockage? Impasse? The terms recur in the context of psychoanalysis and film. It may be that studies in psychoanalysis and cinema will have to broaden its range of reference – certainly, beyond the Freud-Lacan paradigm that, as became clear at key moments in writing this book, continues to hold sway. The pleasures, and anxieties, of looking in cinema have been thoroughly (though by no means exhaustively) explored in terms of voyeurism and sexual difference, identification and narcissism. But it is possible to imagine a new set of questions, and responses, to cinema formulated through the work of a range of psychoanalytic thinkers who have figured hardly at all in contemporary film theory. Think, for example, of D.W. Winnicott's comments on the 'wireless that is left on interminably' – a use of technology that, for Winnicott, amounts to a form of manic, but normal, defence against the feeling of 'death inside', depression (Winnicott 1987: 131). Tantalising – like Christopher Bollas's use of George Romero's *Living Dead* trilogy to describe a patient who, coming into psychoanalysis with only the vestiges of a life, pulls Bollas towards André Green's key theory of the 'dead mother complex' (Bollas 1998: Green 1972). Another point of convergence: cinema and psychoanalysis preoccupied by death, both a means to its divergence.

Studies in psychoanalysis and cinema are now beginning to extend, and diverge, in this way. It remains to be seen what will come of a renewed dialogue between the two.

NOTES

INTRODUCTION

[1] For discussion of models of vision and spectatorship see Crary (1990) and Friedberg (1993).

[2] Schwartz (1999) is an accessible, and readable, discussion of the history of Freud's 'discovery' of psychoanalysis. See, too, Gay (1988).

[3] Denise Riley's *War in the Nursery – Theories of the Child and Mother* offers a powerful analysis of such a connection; D. W. Winnicott's *Home is Where We Start From* is another key text. The connections between the institution(s) of the state and (unconscious) fantasy are also explored in Rose (1993) and Bollas (1994).

[4] The concept of intertextuality has been central to modern film and literary theory. It refers to the network of relations which, because they are forged from a common language – words, images, formal conventions, for example – are profoundly associated with one another. The obvious, and overt, form of this is quotation. See Barthes (1977).

[5] To borrow the title of Stephen Heath's recent account of early psychoanalytic responses to film: see Heath (1999).

[6] On Pabst's *Secrets of a Soul*, see Friedberg (1990); for Hitchcock's relation to psychoanalysis, see Freedman in Freedman and Millington (eds.) (1999).

[7] In 1975, four editors of *Screen* – the journal which did so much to bring psychoanalysis to bear on the study of cinema – expressed their discontent with what could be called a '*Screen* style' of writing. It is a style identified, the editors suggest, by an obscurity which has become a 'particular strategy of writing', and one that 'demoralizes readers'. Commenting on several examples, Buscombe, Gledhill, Lovell and Williams argue instead for a clarity of expression and exposition of the intellectual territory so often taken for granted in some of the contributions to *Screen* (Stephen Heath, Ben Brewster and Colin MacCabe are singled out for special mention). The debate can be followed through the pages of *Screen* or the invaluable collection: *The*

Sexual Subject: A Screen Reader in Sexuality (1992). It is worth noting that, in her introduction to one of the most recent collections on psychoanalysis and cinema, Janet Bergstrom remarks that her readers may be surprised 'to find a directness and lucidity of style and exposition which was not typical of 1970s film theory' (Bergstrom 1999: 6).

[8] See, for example, Maltby (1995); Cook and Bernink (1999); E. Ann Kaplan's introduction to the first edited collection of essays on psychoanalysis and film, *Psychoanalysis and Cinema* (1990); Lapsley and Westlake (1988); Stam (2000); Hayward (1996); Penley (1989); Creed (1993); Cowie (1997) and in Adams and Cowie (1990).

CHAPTER ONE

[1] In 'Cinematic Spectatorship before the Apparatus: The Public Taste for Reality in Fin-de-Siècle Paris', Schwartz presents a fascinating insight into the forms of looking, and technological innovation, which accompanied the development of cinema and cinema spectatorship. Her discussion of the Paris Morgue, and the figure of the dead child, as a key tourist attraction is especially suggestive given the discussion of violence towards children which surrounds the early history of psychoanalysis (Schwartz in Williams (ed.) 1997, pp. 87-94).

[2] 'The Angel in the House' is the title of Coventry Patmore's most famous poem, a nineteenth-century vision of the woman as domestic angel. See Carol Christ's 'Victorian Masculinity and the Angel in the House' for further discussion (Vicinus (ed.) 1977).

[3] For further discussion, see Adams 1996.

[4] The nature of the relationship between Breuer and Anna O., as well as the success, or failure, of her treatment has been the topic of much discussion. See Forrester's excellent 'The true story of Anna O.' (Forrester 1990) and (with caution) Borch-Jacobsen's historical reading of the case, *Remembering Anna O.* (Borch-Jacobsen 1996).

[5] Breuer offers a historical reading of hysteria as a form of feminist protest, a reading which has been central to feminist engagements with the origins of psychoanalysis. For further discussion see Cixous and Clément (1986), Bernheimer and Kahane (1985) and Showalter (1987).

[6] See Siegfried Kracauer's 'The Little Shopgirls Go to the Movies' in Kracauer (1995) and Adorno and Horkheimer's classic vision of the doomed spectator in *Dialectic of Enlightenment* (1979).

[7] Crucially, that wish does not necessarily aim at pleasure – though pleasure, as Constance Penley has pointed out in her important analysis of popular science fiction, can be a requirement of cinema (Penley 1989a). Penley's reading of James Cameron's *The Terminator* is a persuasive example of how psychoanalysis can be brought into contact with popular film. See also Creed (1993 and 1998); Hart (1994).

[8] In fact, commenting on one of his own cases just a few years later, Freud goes so far as to suggest that a patient able to give a coherent account of herself and her symptom could not be a hysteric. 'The patients' inability to give an ordered history of their life in so far as it coincides with the history of their illness,' he insists, 'is characteristic

of the neurosis' (Freud 1905: 16).

⁹ While Breuer comes to the meaning embedded in Anna O.'s delirium by encouraging her to speak, it is Freud who pursues the relation between the two: Anna O. will not speak to just anyone (not even to one of Breuer's colleagues to whom she is otherwise 'devoted' (Freud and Breuer 1895: 31)). In fact, something in his relation to Anna O. proved exhausting, destructive. 'It is impossible,' he recalled, years later, 'for a general practitioner to treat such a case without his activities and way of life being completely destroyed' (cited in Schwartz 1999: 51). The passion, and disturbance, of the speech solicited by this fledgling therapy no doubt plays its part here. Equally, the nature of the attachment between patient and doctor – attachment which does not depend on the use of hypnosis, the relation of submission and authority – is at stake.

¹⁰ See Žižek (2000) for a discussion of cinema as protective fiction in the context of Holocaust comedy.

¹¹ See Penley (1989) and Copjec (1981) for further discussion of this point in film theory.

¹² See Chapter Three, 'Screening Freud' for further discussion of psychoanalysis and its origins in Freud's uncertainty at how to tell the difference between memory and fantasy. It is in terms of a decision between the two that the history of psychoanalysis is often told. Given Freud's attention to the role of memory, the representation of an event to oneself, it has never been that simple. Nevertheless, the polarisation between fantasy and reality continues. On Jeffrey Masson's view, for example, Freud's early 'seduction theory' recognises an 'important truth': 'the sexual, physical and emotional violence that is a real and tragic part of the lives of many children' (Masson 1984: 189). That is, when Freud turns his attention from the effects of seduction to the question of fantasy and the child's unconscious desire, he 'abandons' those who had confided in him the pain of their family histories; 'unforgivable' is Masson's verdict in his first critical work against psychoanalysis, *Freud: The Assault on Truth* (192). Frederick Crews denounces Freud from the other direction: Freud's 'suggestive' treatment, he claims, implanted the idea of abuse in the minds of his gullible patients. Then, he abandoned them (Crews 1997). It is an angry and frustrating debate, which does little justice to the discoveries and doubts pursued through Freud's correspondence with Fliess. At times, the impasse stalls serious engagement with psychoanalysis, though there are ways to rethink it: see Laplanche and Pontalis's 'Fantasy and the Origins of Sexuality' in Burgin et al. (eds.) (1986); Bollas (1995) on the 'imagined and the happened'; Rose (1993).

¹³ In fact, both emotion and gesture had helped to confirm Freud's belief in what his patients were saying. 'The behaviour of patients while they are reproducing these infantile experiences,' he assures the Society for Psychiatry and Neurology in 1896, 'is in every respect incompatible with the assumption that the scenes are anything else than a reality which is being felt with distress and reproduced with the greatest reluctance' (Freud 1896: 204).

CHAPTER TWO

1 Some of Freud's colleagues – notably, Hanns Sachs and Karl Abraham – had more enthusiasm for Pabst's project, its promise to reproduce the experience of psychoanalysis on screen and so to bring Freud's work to public notice. For further discussion see Friedberg (1990); Heath (1999).

2 One of the key thinkers in this tradition is D. W. Winnicott: see Winnicott (1989); Phillips (1988).

3 Creed's analysis is characterised by her attempt to match up the typical fantasies identified by Freud – the primal scene, in which the child watches his or her parents in the act of intercourse, for example – with key sequences from *Alien*. She is also more broadly concerned with the concept of the monstrous-feminine, derived from her readings of Julia Kristeva in the context of contemporary film. See Creed 1993.

4 Baudry's influential essays are included in Mast *et. al.* 1992; for an overview of the debates, see Maltby (1995); Stam (2000). The classic statement on the 'culture industry' and its regressiveness remains Adorno and Horkheimer (1979) [1944].

5 Baudry is borrowing the concept of reality testing from Freud's 'Formulations on the Two Principles of Mental Functioning' (1911, *Standard Edition* XII). The term is introduced to describe the process by which the subject learns to distinguish between internal and external stimuli – between inside and outside of the self. The confusion between the two is, as Laplanche and Pontalis point out, fundamental to hallucination (Laplanche and Pontalis 1973: 382).

6 As Barbara Creed puts it in her introductory essay on 'Film and Psychoanalysis': 'The history of psychoanalytic film theory is complex – partly because it is long and uneven, partly because the theories are difficult, and partly because the evolution of psychoanalytic film theory after the 1970s cannot be understood without recourse to developments in separate, but related areas, such as Althusser's theory of ideology, semiotics, and feminist film theory' (Creed 1998: 77). At the same time, it remains to be seen what would happen if apparatus theory were to be brought into dialogue with the critical theory associated with the Frankfurt School: the pessimistic vision of what, at the beginning of the 1940s, Theodor Adorno and Max Horkheimer describe as the 'culture industry'. The critical theory developed through, and from, Adorno and Horkheimer's *Dialectic of Enlightenment*, written while the authors were in exile in Hollywood and first published in 1944, is a key statement on the culture industry as a powerful source of resistance to social and political change. 'Real life is becoming indistinguishable from the movies,' Adorno and Horkheimer insist, '… the film forces its victims to equate it directly with reality' (Adorno and Horkheimer 1979: 126). It is a bleak vision of cinema as a type of industrialisation of consciousness, the spectator as its victim forced into accepting the truth-value of an oppressive, sometimes even fatal, fiction. It is difficult not to hear a note of panic in this version of cinema as a preoccupying and deadly force – a panic that, for Adorno at least, encompasses psychoanalysis itself as one

more way to occupy men's senses. For further discussion see Lebeau (1995) and Freedman in Freedman and Millington (1999).

[7] The French phrasing – 'un aspect instantané de l'image' – carries the rhetoric of instant photography. Similarly, Lacan's specific use of nourisson, an infant who is not yet weaned from the breast, invokes the image of the mother in the mirror.

[8] See Brennan (1993) for further discussion of Lacan's analysis of the 'modern' ego.

[9] As early as 1952, for example, Frantz Fanon would turn to Lacan's early writings on the mirror stage to account for the scopic regime of racism in European and American culture. The imago of the black man, he argues, turns the black body into the object of a fearful, and hateful, look (cinema provides Fanon with some of his most powerful, and painful, examples) (Fanon 1952). For further discussion, see Marriott (2000); Kaplan (1999); Lebeau (1998). We will also return to the question of the imaginary and aggression in Chapter 5.

[10] See Rose (1976-77: a paper discussed further in Chapter 5); Penley (1989); Copjec (2000).

[11] For a brief account of that 'School' see Laclau's Preface to Žižek's The Sublime Object of Ideology (1989: x).

[12] See Studlar (1988) and Santner (1990) for two important exceptions to this rule.

CHAPTER THREE

[1] The editorial policy followed by Ernst Kris, Marie Bonaparte and Anna Freud (editors of The Origins of Psychoanalysis) has been the subject of much dispute. 'References to sexual traumas occasioned by violent fathers,' Maria Torok states, bluntly, in 1984, 'are omitted'. See Maria Torok, 'Unpublished by Freud to Fliess: Restoring an Oscillation' in Abraham and Torok (1994).

[2] Sartre could not have known it but the question recalls the new motto for psychoanalysis that, in December 1897, Freud proposed to Fliess: 'What have they done to you, you poor child?' – a line from Goethe's well-known lyric, Kennst du das Land? (Masson 1985: 117). The letter was censored in The Origins of Psychoanalysis.

[3] Alfred Hitchcock's Spellbound (1945) – one of the first encounters between psychoanalysis and cinema – is a key example. One climax in the detective plot coincides with the hero's recovery of a childhood memory (his role in the accidental death of his brother). Hitchcock does not seem to have liked his film, celebrated for its innovative dream-sequence with sets designed by Salvador Dali. Unlike Freud, however, Spellbound was a commercial success, helping to generate a popular image of psychoanalysis. Certainly, the American psychoanalytic establishment was interested in the potential of cinema to represent, or misrepresent, its profession. Selznick consulted his own analyst about the film, while Karl Menninger (one of the first supporters of psychoanalysis in the United States) entered into anxious dialogue with Joseph Manckiewicz, David Selznick and May Romm about it. In this sense, Spellbound can be understood as a type of compromise between the institutions of psychoanalysis and cinema (what happens, crudely, if you listen to your analyst rather than to your director?). For further discussion of Hitchcock's

cinema as reflective critique of psychoanalysis, see Freedman (1999).

4 On 28 April 1897, for example, describing the details of a new case to Fliess – 'a young woman whom, for lack of time, I would have preferred to scare off' – Freud offers a sudden insight into the 'dialogue' which, at this point, sustains his method of treatment:

> She came today and confessed that she had thought a lot about the treatment and had discovered an obstacle. 'What is that?' – 'I can make myself out as bad as I must; but I must spare other people. You must allow me to name no names.' – 'No doubt names are unimportant. What you mean are your relations to people. Here it surely will not be possible to conceal anything.' – 'I really mean that earlier I should have been easier to treat than today. Earlier I was unsuspecting; but now the criminal significance of some things has become clear to me and I cannot make up my mind to talk about them.' – 'On the contrary, I believe a mature woman becomes more tolerant about sexual matters.' – 'Yes, you are right there. When I say that the people who are guilty of such things are noble and high-minded I am bound to think that it is a disease, a kind of madness, and I must excuse them.' – 'Well then, let us speak plainly. In my analyses the guilty people are close relatives, father or brother.' – 'Nothing has gone on with my brother.' – 'Your father, then.' And it turned out that her supposedly otherwise noble and respectable father regularly took her to bed when she was from eight to twelve years old and misused her without penetrating ('made her wet,' nocturnal visits). [...] Of course, when I told her that similar and worse things must have happened in her earliest childhood, she could not find it incredible. (Masson 1985: 237-8)

It is a remarkable letter through which the woman's story is heard – until that moment when she would have to describe whatever it was that took place between herself and her father. At that point, it is Freud who takes up the story, paraphrasing for Fliess what his patient has told him. Her voice is now 'off', in brackets – just as Sartre draws a veil over Cäcilie's vision, before bringing her back to the scene of psychoanalysis.

5 See also Diane Waldman and Janet Walker, 'John Huston's *Freud* and Textual Repression: A Psychoanalytic Feminist Reading', in Lehman (1990).

CHAPTER FOUR

1 For further discussion see Jean-Joseph Goux's comparative analysis of the Oedipus myth Goux (1993).

2 To say this is also to shift the focus of an 'applied psychoanalysis', to rule it out, in so far as psychoanalysis shares the terrain of the culture to which it might attempt to apply itself.

3 For further discussion see Irigaray (1985); Lebeau (1995); Butler (1990).

4 Take the *Alien* saga, for example, which, in its scant attention to the vicissitudes of the

heterosexual couple can be said to open up the space for a cinematic vision of the monstrous maternal: from the metaphor of maternity as alien in Ridley Scott's *Alien* to the identification between heroine and monster in *Alien IV* in which the film's 'final girl' (Ripley/Sigourney Weaver) is re-cast as the alien's mother.

[5] It is worth noting Bellour's emphasis on history in this passage – not least because the textual analysis of film to which he contributes so much has sometimes been challenged on the grounds that it obliterates a history of the medium as well as its own theoretical practice. Tom Gunning's bleak reference to 'text-obsessed film analysis' in the course of his fascinating study of film exhibition can stand as one example of such discontent (Gunning 1989: 127). At issue, it seems, are different accounts of the concept of history: Bellour's gesture towards a period roughly defined as modernity is not the localised, situated version of film history that is called for. See Mayne (1993) for further discussion.

[6] See Heath (1999) on cinema's 'platitudinous' representations of psychoanalysis.

CHAPTER FIVE

[1] There have been attempts to shift the dominance of Freud and Lacan in film theory. See, for example, Studlar (1988) for a fascinating study of spectatorship which draws on object-relations theory. More recently, Ayako Saito's contribution to *Endless Nights* (Bergstrom (ed.) (1999)) uses the increasingly influential work of psychoanalyst André Green to move the concept of affect into film studies. A quick glance at the index to the volume, however, suggests that Freud-Lacan still holds sway. Growing interest in the work of Melanie Klein may well begin to shift this (as has happened in literary studies). In particular, the publication of Klein's 'Notes on *Citizen Kane*' (in Phillips and Stonebridge (eds) (1998)) is one starting-point for a consideration of Klein in relation to film.

[2] The script of *Riddles of the Sphinx* was published in *Screen*, Summer 1977, 18, 2.

[3] See Rose (1986); Penley (1989).

[4] See Rose's exploration of femininity, hysteria and spectacle in the nineteenth-century novel, 'George Eliot and the Spectacle of the Woman' in Rose (1986).

[5] For further discussion of this point see Lebeau (1995).

[6] Claire Johnston's quite different approach to Riviere's concept is set out in her 'Femininity and the Masquerade: *Anne of the Indies*', in Kaplan (ed.) (1990).

[7] For a more contextualised discussion of Riviere see 'Negativity in the Work of Melanie Klein' and 'War in the Nursery', in Rose (1993).

[8] See Doane (1987); Brennan (ed.) (1989); Whitford (1991).

[9] It is worth noting that the spectacle of femininity is called upon to mitigate the effects of a prior spectacle of masculinity. For further discussion see Lebeau (1995).

[10] Though Jean Walton's essay includes an important discussion of Klein, her reading of Rivere also comes via Lacan: the question of 'being or having' the phallus structures her account. See Walton (1995)

[11] Elizabeth Abel summarises a familiar set of criticisms at the beginning of 'Race, Class, and Psychoanalysis? Opening Questions': 'The traditional indifference of

psychoanalysis to racial, class and cultural differences, and the tendency of psychoanalysis to insulate subjectivity from social practices and discourses all run contrary to a feminism increasingly attuned to the power of social exigencies and differences in the constitution of subjectivity' (Abel 1990: 184). Similarly, in 'On racism and psychoanalysis', Joel Kovel suggests that the 'great illusion of psychoanalysis, applying to most contemporary discourse no less than the classical Freudian theory, has been to imagine itself free from society as it goes about its work of producing putatively categorical knowledge about the psyche' (Kovel 1995: 205).

[12] For a disturbing account of lynching as spectacle, and the role of photography in the reproduction of a racist vision of the dead black body, see Marriott, '"I'm gonna borrer me a Kodak": Photography and Lynching' in Marriott (2000). Jacqueline Goldsby takes up the relation between visual culture (television, photography) and lynching in the America of the mid-1950s in a powerful analysis of the murder of Emmett Till in 'The High and Low Tech of It: The Meaning of Lynching and the Death of Emmett Till' in Goldsby (1996).

[13] See Bhabha (1994); Mercer (1994); Bergner in Allesandrini (ed.) (1999); Marriott (2000).

[14] There is a long footnote in 'The Negro and Psychopathology' (the controversial chapter on sexuality and racism in *Black Skin, White Masks*) on the theory of the mirror stage set out in Lacan's 'Family Complexes'. These ideas are discussed in more detail in Lebeau (1998).

[15] In the same collection, Gwen Bergner explores Fanon's response to *Home of the Brave* (1949: a film also discussed by Marriott and Kaplan). It is worth noting that Kaplan is putting forward Fanon's traumatic reading of cinema as a counter to what she describes as 'film theory's 1980s Freudian/Lacanian psychoanalytic paradigm of cinema as oedipal regression' (*ibid.*: 149). As an instance of how film theory is turning to the topic of trauma – through *The Freud Scenario*, for example – Kaplan's essay is suggestive, but it is essential, I think, to keep in focus Fanon's re-visioning of Lacan.

[16] Taking its distance from both Metz and Bellour, 'Paranoia and the Film System', first published in *Screen* in 1976-77, remains a key statement of how the image of the woman in cinema takes on the threat of destruction that is the other side of the imaginary pleasures of identification and identity. Returning to Bellour's analysis of the Bodega Bay sequence of *The Birds*, Rose tracks the concept of the imaginary back through Freud and Lacan, uncovering its dynamic of identification, idealisation and aggression. 'Paranoia,' she writes in her opening comments on the psychoanalysis from which film theory borrows its terms, 'is latent to the reversibility of the ego's self-alienation': that is, formed via the subject's identification with an (external) image, the ego is always 'outside' itself, able to become its own object (of love, hate, rivalry) (Rose 1976-77: 88). Following Bellour's account of the role of alternation in the construction of the film narrative, such a reversibility can also be described as internal to the mechanism of film. The basic opposition of shot and counter-shot which sustains the vision of cinema,

Rose concludes, recalls the 'reversal exemplary of the fundamental paradox of identification' (90). It is that reversal which maps cinema onto ego not in terms of a totalising imaginary (the 'spectator centred for mastery' explored by Metz) but of a permanent instability to which *The Birds* bears witness in its spectacular attack on the woman: 'In *The Birds*, the woman is object and cause of the attack' (89). In particular, Rose takes issue with Bellour's reading of the correspondence between Mitch and the gull (Shots 75, 77, 79 and 80):

> At the point where Melanie Daniels is attacked by the gull, the analysis iden-
> tifies the attack with the reciprocal gaze of Mitch Brenner whose dominant
> mobility has determined the structure of the preceding shots of the sequence.
> The gull therefore represents a type of male violation. But this identification
> is challenged by the fact that Melanie sees Mitch but does not see the gull,
> which is shown in an anticipatory shot presented only to the spectator. The
> introduction of an object which is not seen reintroduces the elision of the
> subject's centrality which we have found to be latent to the opposition itself,
> but it leaves the gull without cause, unless the latter can be read in the
> meeting of looks which syntagmatically generates the attack. The gull would
> not in that case represent an active male sexuality, but the suspension of its
> possibility ... which shows, firstly, that the aggressivity is a function of the
> alternation and not derived from one of its terms. (Rose 1976-77)

Very much inside the exchange of looks which generates the narrative of *The Birds*, Rose halts the movement of the film at the point at which the system of alternation identified by Bellour – 'Melanie seeing/what Melanie sees' – breaks down. Melanie does not see the gull which is about to attack her; she is decentred from, and by, the narrative – a decentring that, recalling the 'elision' (absence, division) of the subject in the mirror, appears to make her available for attack. In other words, Melanie comes to stand in for the subject alienated through the process of identification with an image ('the elision of the subject's centrality which we have found to be latent to the opposition itself') at the level of both film narrative (she is attacked) and film code: the alternation of seeing/seen breaks down at the moment of attack as Melanie becomes the object of a look that she has not seen. See Penley (1989) for further discussion of the differences between Rose and Bellour.

BIBLIOGRAPHY

Abel, E. (1990) 'Race, Class and Psychoanalysis? Opening Questions', in M. Hirsch and E. F. Keller (eds) *Conflicts in Feminism*. London and New York: Routledge, 184-204.

Abraham, N. and M. Torok (1994) *The Shell and the Kernel* (Vol. 1) (Trans. N. T. Rand). Chicago and London: University of Chicago Press.

Adams, P. (1996) *The Emptiness of the Image: Psychoanalysis and Sexual Difference*. London and New York: Routledge.

Adams, P. and E. Cowie (eds) (1990) *The Woman in Question*. London and New York: Verso.

Adorno, T. (1991) *The Culture Industry*. London: Routledge.

Adorno, T. and M. Horkheimer (1979) *Dialectic of Enlightenment* (Trans. J. Cumming). London: Verso.

Alessandrini, A. C. (ed.) (1999) *Frantz Fanon: Critical Perspectives*. London and New York: Routledge.

Andreas-Salomé, L. (1987) *The Freud Journal*. London: Quartet Books.

Anzieu, D. (1986) *Freud's Self-Analysis*. London: The Hogarth Press.

Appignanesi, L. and J. Forrester (1992) *Freud's Women*. London: Weidenfeld and Nicolson.

Barthes, R. (1973) 'Textual Analysis: Poe's "Valdemar"', in D. Lodge (ed.) (1988) *Modern Criticism and Theory: A Reader*. London and New York: Longman, 172-95.

_____ (1977) 'From Work to Text', in *Image, Music, Text* (Trans. S. Heath). London: Fontana, 159.

Baudry, J-L. (1992) 'Ideological Effects of the Basic Cinematographic Apparatus', in G. Mast *et al.* (eds) *Film Theory and Criticism*. New York and Oxford: Oxford University Press, 302-12.

Bazin, A. (1967) 'The Ontology of the Photographic Image', in *What is Cinema?* Berkeley, LA and London: University of California Press, 9-16.

Bellour, R. (2000) *The Analysis of Film*. Bloomington and Indianapolis: Indiana University Press.

Bergstrom, J. (ed.) (1999) *Endless Night: Cinema and Psychoanalysis, Parallel Histories*. Berkeley: University of California Press.

Bergstom, J. and M. A. Doane (eds) (1989) 'The Spectatrix', *Camera Obscura*, 20-1.

Bernheimer, C. and C. Kahane (eds) (1985) *In Dora's Case*. London: Virago.

Bhabha, H. K. (1994) *The Location of Culture*. London and New York: Routledge.

Bollas, C. (1994) *Being a Character: Psychoanalysis and Self Experience*. London: Routledge.

_____ (1995) *Cracking Up: The Work of Unconscious Experience*. London: Routledge.

Borch-Jacobsen, M. (1989) *The Freudian Subject* (Trans. C. Porter). London: Macmillan.

_____ (1996) *Remembering Anna O.: A Century of Mystification*. London and New York: Routledge.

Brennan, T. (ed.) (1989) *Between Feminism and Psychoanalysis*. London and New York: Routledge.

_____ (1993) *History After Lacan*. London and New York: Routledge.

Burch, N. (1990) *Life to those Shadows* (Trans. B. Brewster). London: BFI.

Burgin V., J. Donald, and C. Kaplan (eds) (1986) *Formations of Fantasy*. London and New York: Methuen.

Butler, J. (1990) *Gender Trouble: Feminism and the Subversion of Identity*. London and New York: Routledge.

Campbell, J. and J. Harbord (eds) (1998) *Psycho-politics and Cultural Desires*. London: UCL Press.

Cixous, H. and C. Clement (1986) *The Newly Born Woman* (Trans. B. Wing). Manchester: Manchester University Press.

Clover, C. (1989) 'Her Body, Himself: Gender in the Slasher Film', in J. Donald (ed.) *Fantasy and the Cinema*. London: BFI, 91-135.

Cohen, M. and L. Braudy (1992) 'The Apparatus', in G. Mast *et al.* (eds) *Film Theory and Criticism*. New York and Oxford: Oxford University Press, 690-707.

Cook, P. and M. Bernink (eds) (1999) *The Cinema Book* (2nd edn.). London: BFI.

Copjec, J. (1981) '"*India Song/Son nom de Venise dans Calcutta désert*": The Compulsion to Repeat', *October*, 17.

_____ (ed.) (1994) *Supposing the Subject*. London and New York: Verso.

_____ (2000) 'The Orthopsychic Subject: Film Theory and the Reception of Lacan', in R. Stam and T. Miller (eds) *Film and Theory: Anthology*. Oxford: Blackwell, 437-455.

Cowie, E. (1997) *Representing the Woman: Cinema and Psychoanalysis*. Basingstoke: Macmillan.

Crary, J. (1990) *Techniques of the Observer: On Vision and Modernity in the Nineteenth Century*. Massachusetts and London: MIT Press.

Creed, B. (1989) 'Horror and the Monstrous-Feminine: An Imaginary Abjection', in J. Donald (ed.) *Fantasy and the Cinema*. London: BFI, 63-90.

_____ (1993) *The Monstrous-Feminine: Film, Feminism and Psychoanalysis*. London: Routledge.

_____ (1998) 'Film and Psychoanalysis', in J. Hill and P. C. Gibson (eds) *The Oxford Guide to Film Studies*. Oxford: Oxford University Press, 77-90.

Crews, F. *et al.* (1997) *The Memory Wars: Freud's Legacy in Dispute*. London: Granta Books.

David-Ménard, M. (1989) *Hysteria from Freud to Lacan* (Trans. C. Porter). Cornell: Cornell

University Press.

Doane, M. A. (1987) *The Desire to Desire: The Woman's Film of the 1940s*. London: Macmillan.

____ (1991) *Femmes Fatales*. London and New York: Routledge.

____ (2000) 'Film and the Masquerade: Theorizing the Female Spectator', in R. Stam and T. Miller (eds) *Film and Theory: An Anthology*. Oxford: Blackwell, 495-509.

Donald, J., A. Friedberg, and L. Marcus (eds) (1998) *Close Up: 1927-1933. Cinema and Modernism*. London: Cassell.

Dowd Hall, J. (1983) '"The Mind that Burns in Each Body": Women, Rape, and Racial Violence', in A. Snitow, C. Stansell and S. Thompson (eds) *Desire: The Politics of Sexuality*. London: Virago, 339-360.

Elliott, A. (1994) *Psychoanalytic Theory: An Introduction*. Oxford: Blackwell.

Elliott, A. and S. Frosh (eds) (1995) *Psychoanalysis in Contexts: Paths between Theory and Modern Culture*. London and New York: Routledge.

Elsaesser, T. (ed.) (1990) *Early Cinema: Space, Frame, Narrative*. London: BFI.

Fanon, F. (1986) *Black Skin, White Masks* (Trans. C. L. Markmann). London: Pluto Press.

Felman, S. (ed.) *Literature and Psychoanalysis: The Question of Reading Otherwise*. Baltimore: John Hopkins University Press.

Ferguson, H. (1996) *The Lure of Dreams: Sigmund Freud and the Construction of Modernity*. London and New York: Routledge.

Fisher, D. J. (1999) 'Sartre's Freud: Dimensions of Intersubjectivity in *The Freud Scenario*', in J. Bergstrom (ed.) *Endless Night: Cinema and Psychoanalysis, Parallel Histories*. Berkeley: University of California Press, 126-152.

Forrester, J. (1990) *The Seductions of Psychoanalysis: Freud, Lacan and Derrida*. Cambridge: Cambridge University Press.

Freedman, J. and R. Millington (eds) (1999) *Hitchcock's America*. New York and Oxford: Oxford University Press.

Freud, Sigmund (1886) 'Report on my Studies in Paris and Berlin', *The Standard Edition of the Complete Psychological Works Sigmund Freud* (hereafter *SE*) (1886-1889). London: The Hogarth Press and The Institute of Psycho-Analysis, 1-16.

____ (1888) 'Hysteria', *SE I*, 37-62.

____ (1888-93) 'Some Points for a Comparative Study of Organic and Hysterical Motor Paralyses', *SE I*, 155-72.

____ (1892-94) 'Preface and Footnotes to the Translation of Charcot's *Tuesday Lectures*', *SE I*, 129-46.

____ (1893) 'Charcot', *SE III* (1893-1899), 7-24.

____ (1896) 'The Aetiology of Hysteria', *SE III* (1893-1899), 187-222.

____ (1900) *The Interpretation of Dreams. SE IV and V* (1900-1901).

____ (1905) 'Fragment of an Analysis of a Case of Hysteria' ('Dora'), *SE VII* (1901-1905), 1-122.

____ (1908) 'Creative Writers and Day-Dreaming', *SE IX* (1906-1908), 141-54.

____ (1910) 'A Special Type of Choice of Object Made by Men (Contributions to the Psychology of Love I), *SE XI* (1910), 163-76.

____ (1919) 'The Uncanny', *SE XVII* (1917-1919), 217-56.

____ (1921) 'Group Psychology and the Analysis of the Ego', *SE XVIII* (1920-1922), 65-144.

____ (1925) 'An Autobiographical Study', *SE XX* (1925-1926), 1-74.

____ (1925a) 'Some Psychical Consequences of the Anatomical Distinction Between the Sexes', *SE XIX* (1923-1925), 241-60.

____ (1926) 'The Question of Lay Analysis', *SE XX* (1925-1926), 177-258.

____ (1927) 'Fetishism', *SE XXI* (1927-1931), 147-58.

____ (1931) 'Female Sexuality', *SE XXI*, 221-46.

____ (1933) 'Femininity', *SE XXII* (1932-1936), 112-35.

____ (1940) 'Splitting of the Ego in the Process of Defence', *SE XXIII* (1937-1939), 271-8.

____ (1992) *Letters of Sigmund Freud* (Trans. T. and J. Stern) (Ernst L. Freud (ed.)) New York: Dover.

Freud, S. and J. Breuer (1895) *Studies on Hysteria. SE II* (1893-1895), 1-306.

Friedberg, A. (1993) *Window Shopping: Cinema and the Postmodern*. Berkeley and Los Angeles: University of California Press.

____ (1990) 'An *Unheimlich* Maneuver between Psychoanalysis and the Cinema: *Secrets of a Soul* (1926), in E. Rentschler (ed.) *The Films of G. W. Pabst: An Extraterritorial Cinema*. New Brunswick and London: Rutgers University Press, 41-51.

Gabbard, K. and G. O. Gabbard (1987) *Psychiatry and the Cinema*. Chicago and London: The University of Chicago Press.

Gay, P. (1988) *Freud: A Life for Our Time*. London: Papermac.

Gelfand, T. (1988) '"Mon Cher Docteur Freud": Charcot's Unpublished Correspondence to Freud, 1888-1893', in *Bulletin of the History of Medicine* LXII, 563-88.

Goldsby, J. (1996) 'The High and Low Tech of It: The Meaning of Lynching and the Death of Emmett Till', in *The Yale Journal of Criticism*, 9, 2, 245-82.

Goux, J-J. (1993) *Oedipus, Philosopher* (Trans. C. Porter). Stanford, CA: Stanford University Press.

Green, A. (1972) *On Private Madness*. London: Hogarth Press.

Gunning, T. (1997) 'An Aesthetic of Astonishment: Early Film and the (In)Credulous Spectator', in L. Williams (ed.) *Viewing Positions: Ways of Seeing Film*. New Brunswick, New Jersey: Rutgers University Press, 114-33.

Hall, S. (1996) 'The After-Life of Frantz Fanon? Why Now? Why *Black Skin, White Masks*?', in A. Read (ed.) *The Fact of Blackness: Frantz Fanon and Visual Representation*. Seattle: Bay Press, 12-37.

Hansen, M. (1986) 'Pleasure, Ambivalence and Identification: Valentino and Female Spectatorship', in *Cinema Journal,* 25 (4), 6-32.

Hart, L. (1994) *Fatal Women: Lesbian Sexuality and the Mark of Aggression*. London and New York: Routledge.

Hayward, S. (1996) *Key Concepts in Cinema Studies*. London and New York: Routledge.

Heath, S. (1981) *Questions of Cinema*. London: Macmillan.

____ (1986) 'Joan Riviere and the Masquerade', in V. Burgin, J. Donald and C. Kaplan (eds) *Formations of Fantasy*. London and New York: Methuen, 45-61.

____ (1992) 'Difference', in *The Sexual Subject: A Screen Reader in Sexuality*. London and New York: Routledge, 47-106.

____ (1999) 'Cinema and Psychoanalysis: Parallel Histories', in J. Bergstrom (ed.) *Endless Night: Cinema and Psychoanalysis, Parallel Histories*. Berkeley: University of California Press, 25-56.

Hirschmüller, A. (1978) *The Life and Work of Josef Breuer: Physiology and Psychoanalysis*. New York and London: New York University Press.

Irigaray, L. (1985) *Speculum of the Other Woman* (Trans. G. C. Gill). New York: Cornell University Press.

Kaplan, E. Ann (ed.) (1990) *Psychoanalysis and Cinema*. London and New York: Routledge.

____ (1999) 'Fanon, trauma and cinema', in A. C. Alessandrini (ed.) *Frantz Fanon: Critical Perspectives*. London and New York: Routledge, 146-58.

Kirby, L. (1997) *Parallel Tracks: The Railroad and Silent Cinema*. Devon: University of Exeter Press.

Kittler, F. (1997) 'Romanticism-Psychoanalysis-Film: A History of the Double', in *Literature, media, informations systems*. Amsterdam: Overseas Publishers Association, 85-100.

Kovel, J. (1988) *White Racism*. London: Free Association Books.

Kracauer, S. (1947) *From Caligari to Hitler: A Psychological History of the German Film*. Princeton: Princeton University Press.

____ (1995) *The Mass Ornament: Weimar Essays* (Trans. T .Y. Levin). Cambridge, Massachusetts and London, England: Harvard University Press.

Kristeva, J. (1986) *The Kristeva Reader*. Oxford: Basil Blackwell.

Lacan, J. (1977) *Écrits: A selection* (Trans. A. Sheridan). London: Tavistock Publications.

____ (1979) *The Four Fundamental Concepts of Psycho-Analysis* (Trans. A. Sheridan). Harmondsworth, Middlesex: Penguin.

____ (1988) *The Seminar of Jacques Lacan. Book I: Freud's Papers on Technique 1953-1954* (Trans. J. Forrester). Cambridge: Cambridge University Press.

Laplanche, J. (1989) *New Foundations for Psychoanalysis* (Trans. D. Macey). Oxford: Blackwell.

Laplanche, J. and J. B. Pontalis (1973) *The Language of Psychoanalysis*. London: Karnac Books.

____ (1986) 'Fantasy and the Origins of Sexuality', in V. Burgin, J. Donald and C. Kaplan (eds) *Formations of Fantasy*. London and New York: Methuen, 5-34.

Lapsley, R. and M. Westlake (1988) *Film Theory: An Introduction*. Manchester: Manchester University Press.

Lebeau V. (1995) *Lost Angels: Psychoanalysis and Cinema*. London and New York: Routledge.

____ (1998) 'Psychopolitics: Frantz Fanon's *Black Skin, White Masks*', in J. Campbell and Harbord (eds) *Psycho-Politics and Cultural Desires*. London: UCL Press, 113-23.

Lehman, P. (ed.) (1990) *Close Viewings*. Florida: Florida State University Press.

Maltby, R. (1995) *Hollywood Cinema*. Oxford: Blackwell.

Marriott, D. (2000) *On Black Men*. Edinburgh: Edinburgh University Press.

Masson, J-M. (1984) *Freud: The Assault on Truth: Freud's Suppression of the Seduction Theory*. London and Boston: Faber and Faber.

_____ (1985) *The Complete Letters of Sigmund Freud to Wilhelm Fliess 1887-1904* (Trans. J-M. Masson). Cambridge MA and London: The Belknap Press.

Mast, G. *et al.* (eds.) *Film Theory and Criticism*. New York and Oxford: Oxford University Press.

Mayne, J. (1993) *Cinema and Spectatorship*. London and New York: Routledge.

McGrath, W. J. (1986) *Freud's Discovery of Psychoanalysis: The Politics of Hysteria*. London: Cornell University Press.

Mercer, K. (1994) *Welcome to the Jungle*. London: Routledge.

Metz, C. (1982) *Psychoanalysis and Cinema: The Imaginary Signifier*. London: Macmillan.

Mitchell, J. (1974) *Psychoanalysis and Feminism*. London: Allen Lane.

Mitchell, J. and J. Rose (eds) (1982) *Feminine Sexuality: Jacques Lacan and the École freudienne* (Trans. J. Rose). London: Macmillan.

Montrelay, M. (1978) 'Inquiry into Femininity', in P. Adams and E. Cowie (eds) (1990) *The Woman in Question*. London and New York: Verso, 253-72.

Mulvey, L. (1992) 'Visual Pleasure and Narrative Cinema', in *The Sexual Subject: A Screen Reader in Sexuality*. London and New York: Routledge, 22-34.

Munsterberg, H. (1970) *The Film: A Psychological Study of the Silent Photoplay in 1916*. New York: Dover.

Penley, C. (1989) *The Future of an Illusion: Film, Feminism, and Psychoanalysis*. London: Routledge.

_____ (1989a) 'Time Travel, Primal Scene and the Critical Dystopia', in J. Donald (ed.) *Fantasy and the Cinema*. London: BFI, 197-212.

Phillips, A. (1988) *Winnicott*. London: Fontana Press.

_____ (1998) *The Beast in the Nursery*. London: Faber and Faber.

Phillips, J. and L. Stonebridge (eds) (1998) *Reading Melanie Klein*. London and New York: Routledge.

Pontalis, J. B. (1981) *Frontiers in Psychoanalysis. Between the Dream and Psychic Pain* (Trans. C. and P. Cullen). London: The Hogarth Press and the Institute of Psycho-Analysis.

Popple, S. (1996) 'The Diffuse Beam: Cinema and Change', in C. Williams (ed.) *Cinema: the Beginnings and the Future*. London: University of Westminster Press, 82-99.

Powdermaker, H. (1950) *Hollywood the Dream Factory: An Anthropologist Looks at the Movie Makers*. London: Secker and Warburg.

Rank, O. (1971) *The Double: A Psychoanalytic Study*. London: Karnac Books.

Riley, D. (1983) *War in the Nursery – Theories of the Child and Mother*. London: Virago.

Riviere, J. (1986) 'Womanliness as a Masquerade', in V. Burgin, J. Donald and C. Kaplan (eds) *Formations of Fantasy*. London: Routledge.

Robinson, D. (1996) 'Realising the Vision: 300 Years of Cinematography', in C. Williams (ed.) *Cinema: the Beginnings and the Future*, London: University of Westminster Press, 1-25.

Rose, J. (1976-1977) 'Paranoia and the Film System', in *Screen* 1976-1977, 17, 4, 85-104.

____ (1986) *Sexuality in the Field of Vision*. London: Verso.

____ (1993) *Why War? - Psychoanalysis, Politics, and the Return to Melanie Klein*. Oxford: Basil Blackwell.

Roudinesco, E. (1997) *Jacques Lacan* (Trans. Barbara Bray). Cambridge: Polity Press.

Sadoul, G. (1973) *Histoire Générale du Cinéma* (6 volumes). Paris: Denoël.

Santner, E. (1990) *Stranded Objects: Mourning, Memory and Film in Postwar Germany*. Ithaca: Cornell University Press.

Sartre, J-P. (1985) *The Freud Scenario*. Chicago: The University of Chicago Press.

Schwartz, J. (1999) *Cassandra's Daughter: A History of Psychoanalysis in Europe and America*. Middlesex: Penguin.

Showalter, E. (1987) *The Female Malady*. London: Virago.

Stacey, J. (1987) 'Desperately Seeking Difference', in *Screen* 28 (1), 48-61.

Stam, R. (2000) *Film Theory: An Introduction*. Oxford: Blackwell.

Stam, R. and T. Miller (2000) *Film and Theory: An Anthology*. Oxford: Blackwell.

Studlar, G. (1988) *In the Realm of Pleasure: Von Sternberg, Dietrich, and the Masochistic Aesthetic*. Urbana: University of Illinois Press.

Tustin, F. (1992) *Autistic States in Children* (Rev. edn.). London and New York: Tavistock/ Routledge.

Veith, I. (1965) *Hysteria: The History of a Disease*. Chicago: Chicago University Press.

Vicinus, M. (ed.) (1977) *A Widening Sphere: Changing Roles of Victorian Women*. London: Methuen.

Walker, A. (1986) *You Can't Keep a Good Woman Down*. London: The Woman's Press.

Walker, J. (1999) 'Textual Trauma in *Kings Row* and *Freud*', in J. Bergstrom (ed.) *Endless Night: Cinema and Psychoanalysis, Parallel Histories*. Berkeley: University of California Press.

Walton, J. (1995) 'Re-Placing Race in (White) Psychoanalytic Discourse: Founding Narratives of Feminism', *Critical Inquiry*, 21, 775-804.

Whitford, M. (1991) *Luce Irigaray: Philosophy in the Feminine*. London and New York: Routledge.

Williams, L. (ed.) (1997) *Viewing Positions: Ways of Seeing Film*. New Brunswick: Rutgers University Press.

Winnicott, D. W. (1987) *Through Paediatrics to Psychoanalysis: Collected Papers*. London: Karnac Books.

____ (1989) *Playing and Reality*. London and New York: Routledge.

____ (1990) *Home is Where We Start From: Essays be a psychoanalyst* (C. Winnicott, R. Shepherd and M. Davis (eds) Middlesex: Penguin.

Wollen, P. (1999) 'Freud as Adventurer', in J. Bergstrom (ed.) *Endless Night: Cinema and Psychoanalysis, Parallel Histories*. Berkeley: University of California Press, 153-70.

Wright, E. and E. Wright (eds) (1999) *The Žižek Reader*. Oxford: Blackwell.

Žižek, S. (1989) *The Sublime Object of Ideology*. London: Verso

INDEX